MW01194286

Brotherhood

&

The Sun Papers

(2 Books)

Joseph Benner

2017 by McAllister Editions (MCALLISTEREDITIONS@GMAIL.COM). This book is a classic, and a product of its time. It does not reflect the same views on race, gender, sexuality, ethnicity, and interpersonal relations as it would if it was written today.

CONTENTS

BOOK ONE
BROTHERHOOD

AN IMPERSONAL MESSAGE

1. THE VOICE

YOU who have reached that stage in your climb to the heights where you are no longer seeking anything of self, having tasted of all that the outer world and its human teachers can offer, and something within is strongly insisting that you begin to prove and demonstrate what you have learned by living it and using it to help others who are still seeking;

You, who have felt within the heart a definite call to service and yearn to follow and obey, but who from obeying many urges in the past, only to be disappointed and disillusioned each time by failure of the leaders to be worthy of the Causes they represent, and you are therefore uncertain about this call, and are fearful of not knowing just what you ought to and can do;

You who have not yet had this experience, but who are moved by a strong loving desire to help lift the load from those less fortunately situated, and who would know what is that insistent something within, and whose the voice that thus calls;

Know, one and all, what you feel is My Love quickening into conscious active life in your heart, and what you hear is My Voice calling you to make ready for the Work I have been preparing you for — a Work that is your Work, long waiting for you to do, — when you have proven that self is no longer in control, and that you are willing to let Me lead the remainder of the way.

You who think you are now ready, and sincerely wish to follow, hear this My Word and seek prayerfully to know My full meaning.

First, remember who I am, I who am in all men, Who am That which speaks through all men, Who am the Self of you who read, dwelling deep within the heart — the innermost of you, and Who seek to come forth as the Christ and to show *Myself* — your Highest Self — to all men.

Remember that I always speak from out the heart, and not from the head, the intellect being but My servant, My interpreter. But when the servant acknowledges not his Master, having grown proud, and deems himself above his station and tries to impress others with his knowledge and importance, then you may know why it is so hard to hear *My* voice and to know when it is I speaking, and why you become so often confused and so uncertain what to do. Therefore it is most necessary that you determine whence comes the voice or voices that so confuse and disturb you.

But, you say, suppose you have not yet reached the stage where you are able actually to hear a voice speaking within and to know it as one assuming to teach or lead you.

Know that it is not an actual voice such as your physical ears hear that speaks; for are not every desire, every urge, every hope, longing, fear, discouragement, anxiety, regret, voices heard just as surely and effectively as audible voices?

And while all such are voices I use to teach you the right from the wrong way, yet My Voice, that you long so to hear and to be always sure is Mine, you will never truly hear and know until you let Love abide and rule in your heart. For Love alone can clear away that in your heart and consciousness which causes you to listen to the voice of self, thus preventing your hearing Me when I speak.

But know, My Child, there are sure ways of knowing when the voice of self speaks, and when I speak — to him who sincerely wills to know, and who is ready to face self, and see and know it for just what it is, and just what it pretends to be and is not.

Self is always in an attitude of fighting for and protecting its own, always afraid of losing something it possesses; and so its voices of criticism, condemnation, anxiety, fear, worry, selfishness, greed, envy, jealousy are ever heard in their efforts to hold your attention; while My Voice of Love and Faith, Hope and Trust, Understanding and Discrimination always seeks to enlist your interest in the Truth I would unfold to you.

The voice of self is always asking, demanding something for self, is always concerned solely with self. My Voice always points you to and concerns you with others whom I want you to think of and to help.

The voice of self sounds from without, always relates to something in the outer world, or to conditions springing from it. My Voice always sounds from within, relating to things of the Soul-state, your Soul, or your brother's.

The voice of self ever seeks by much reasoning and argument to oppose anything that would deprive the self of some power or prerogative long held or exercised by it. My Voice speaks from deep within the heart and declares the Truth so definitely that unless self has complete control, the mind cannot but accept and recognize it as Truth.

The voice of self is always trying to get from others that which will benefit self, often hiding such benefit behind sophistries put forth to fool the mind into believing they are for others' good. My Voice definitely requires that you denounce the ways of self, that you realize now and always that My Way is just the opposite of that of self; for it is ever the way of loving service to others, instead of getting for self.

Especially would I have you know that any voice that holds out to you any way of gaining knowledge or power at a price other than through earnest seeking first My Kingdom and living the life of My Son is the voice of self, no matter if spoken by those proclaimed to be great teachers, swamis, yogis, initiates, or masters, and no matter how much they charge for their teachings. For the Way unto Me cannot be found except as My Son Jesus taught and lived — the Way of loving service to others and the crucifixion of self.

Many have thought they heard My Voice spoken by such teachers, only to learn what my real Voice finally making itself heard in the heart clearly pointed out — that self both within the teachers and within themselves cared nothing for Me, but only for what it could gain for self, and that it was only head knowledge that was being taught, and that it contained no spiritual life, and hence no real power came with it.

Finally, you can always tell when it is *not* My Voice that speaks; for whenever anything is said that is not wholly good, that is not spoken in love, that is not as you know God would say and inspire it, then you may know it is self, trying to keep your mind "separate" so it cannot hear My Voice when I would lead it back to the consciousness of Me.

2. THE CALL TO SERVICE

WHEN a message comes containing an opportunity for real service, and disclosing a real plan and a real work for the helping of your brothers; not some vague highsounding ideal, but a definite practical work that your Soul recognizes, and your heart leaps toward in glad response — know that such response is My Voice calling you to the Work I have been preparing you for, and you need not question or doubt, for your Soul commands you to obey.

But if there is no glad response in your heart, not even a faint voice there calling upon you to investigate as there may be something in this for you — and instead there is only a coldness and an entire lack of interest — know that message is for others and that particular Work is not for you, for you could be of no assistance, not being ready for such Work — as yet.

But if hearing, and at first thus happily responding, if but for a moment, before doubts crowd in and from outer sources come advice and argument, criticism of that particular work or of the way it came to you, or of the messenger who brought it, fast smothering the urge in the heart still trying to hold your attention, know that I am but trying and testing you, to see if you are as yet ready for the Work which I always have awaiting My proven and faithful servants; to see if I can use you to awaken and prepare my other children so I can unfold My nature in them that they can feel Me as the Love in their hearts, and can thereby hear My voice there, and know I am their Higher and Real Self and that I am calling them also, anxious to lead them forth into the New Day.

While all calls are My Call, each with its separate appeal, yet each is but leading you on to a realization that all outer things that appeal, all calls of ambition, of riches, of leadership, of power, of human love, yea even of Spiritual attainment, are but the allurements of the separate self, that I use to build Me a strong personality in you, with its power of concentration and ability to accomplish; an instrument I thus develop and prepare for use in the fulfillment of My Plan and Purpose. Then when all is ready, in order that there may be nothing to interfere with or hinder Me in such use, one by one I take from you all outer things that still allure, until there is nothing anymore left, nothing and no one you can look or turn to but Me, — and you have learned to want and to know Me as the one and only thing of importance, and the perfect serving of Me becomes the sole concern and ambition of your life.

It is then only I can send you the Great Call and you can hear it *in your heart*, which now has been opened wide for My use alone, and has been cleansed of all desires of self. Then only can you hear that Call, the call to My blessed ones, those who have dedicated themselves to Me and now live only to serve Me in their brothers.

To all such of you, for there are many whom I have so prepared and who have responded, and who are working selflessly as one with Me, I now send the Call to Service, the call to join the Great Brotherhood of Servers; and those who hear and who know My voice and who gladly have learned to heed it, I am opening their eyes and permitting them a vision of My Plan and of My Purpose for the New Age you are now entering, and am enabling them to comprehend the true and glorious meaning of Brotherhood, that Brotherhood I intend soon to bring forth from the Kingdom within, into actual manifestation in men's midst.

Those of you who refuse to align yourselves with others, thinking that unnecessary for you can come to Me direct, and get all the guidance and help you need, — know you are still thinking of self and are not yet ready for true Service. To you I say the days of seeking and getting for self are past — never to return. No more studying to attain powers will I allow. The training period I allotted for such purpose is over. If you but know it, you brought all the "powers" you seek along with you. And I have been trying to teach you in the school of life's experiences and under those I appointed for your discipline and training, that when you are ready to use these powers — which in reality are not yours but Mine — no longer for selfish purposes, but wholly in My Service, I will uncover them to your consciousness and direct you perfectly in their use.

For the Force I formerly gave to man for the growth and development of self is now withdrawn. Henceforth all My Wisdom, Love and Power is poured into and through the Great Brotherhood of the Spirit. He who would receive must go within his heart and find Me as the Christ, His Higher Self, abiding there, and must give up all of personal self and follow Him, must enlist and serve under His banner — the banner of Brotherhood.

It is true you can still come to Me and get the guidance you need, but only for the use and helping of your fellowmen. No more will I give of My Force to develop the consciousness of the separate self. Now all must go to the use of the Christ — to the binding and lifting of all self-consciousness into the consciousness of Brotherhood.

I now call upon you to *live* and *use* what you so long have been studying and believing with your intellect about Service and Brotherhood. When you believe in your heart, which belief can only come from USE and DEMONSTRATION, then you will truly *BE* and *KNOW* a *Brother*, and not before. Only you who forget and are no longer concerned with your Soul's status can truly serve Me in your brothers, for when you learn to love your brothers more than self, then you will hear My Voice speaking in your heart telling you what to do and how to do it.

Those who do not want to acknowledge any leader other than their Higher Self and therefore fear to join others in service in outer organizations, thinking such cannot be impersonally or spiritually directed by any human personality, — know that you are indeed striving to obey the voice of your Soul, but ignorantly; for your Soul will never require you to acknowledge or obey any leader who would ask you to do anything to which your Higher Self would not assent. Any such command or requirement of such a leader would immediately absolve you from allegiance in any such organization. But Wisdom also would first require you fully to satisfy your mind as to your Soul's desire, as previously explained, regarding the Call to such Service. For can you not realize, that all that has gone before, My bringing you through so many disappointments and disillusionments, through all the various experiences and teachings into a consciousness of Me, as your Higher and only Self, has been but to lead you into that wider and deeper consciousness of Me *as the Higher Self also of your brother*, and that you and your brother thus *become one in Me*, and that *there is and can be no separation*. That is the true vision of Brotherhood. When you have caught that, then you have entered the Kingdom of My Consciousness and see and know as I would have you see and know.

Therefore there cannot possibly be any separation between those consecrated to the Vision, — all are one, whether in the Spirit or in the flesh, — they are a part of that Great White Brotherhood of Spirit, the most perfect organization that is, for It is Eternal, always was, and always will be; and It is gradually drawing to Itself — one by one — all who have learned and conquered the illusion of self and separation.

Do you want to be separate any more, My children, now that you know the Truth? No, for from now on the great hunger of your life will be for *conscious* union with your Brothers; for only then will you find and truly and fully know Me.

As to any outer organization representing My Kingdom of the Spirit down in the midst of men being directed by a human personality, know that only through human instruments can My Will be done on earth. Even as I can accomplish My Will in large ways by inspiring many minds with My Love through My Spirit — the Christ — within them, so do I inspire many to look only within to Him for leadership, — so that they may realize that He in them and He in every one of their brothers is One — is I, their True and Only Self. Therefore it is not the personality of such leader they see any more, but only the Master — the Christ — of such personality through whom I work.

Many have thus become His proven and faithful Disciples, My Beloved Sons, and they gladly obey His commands, knowing Him only as their Higher Self, and living only to help others also thus to learn to know and to obey Him; and they, through such selfless love and consequent oneness of purpose as His followers, thus become banded in Spirit in a great army of workers for Him. And all who can similarly learn to follow and serve Him, automatically become one of this invisible army, all under His leadership, and of course guided and directed by His more tested and proven ones — your elder Brothers — My generals and lieutenants, in mundane army terms. And how may you know your elder Brothers, those I have chosen to lead and guide My children into the New Day? By one way only — by that most sure way — by their fruits, by compelling others by their lives and their achievements to recognize the Christ of them.

As in the past they have not been called from the high places, but I have called again the fishers of men — those whose lives are consecrated to the uplifting and helping of their fellows — particularly those who have not sought for self, but only to serve the Christ in their brothers, those whose names are unknown to the outer world for the work they have done, but who have brought thousands and thousands into the consciousness of Me in their hearts, each in his own way.

Think you I can work My will otherwise? It is only through such chosen ones — they who have given themselves over wholly to Me — that I can do My Will upon the earth as I purpose it to be done. To such I give a glimpse of My Plan and My purpose. But think not I work only through such conscious channels. Am I not working My Will through you, and through every one who at any time seeks to obey his Highest Self? Such, in very truth, form My Army — My workers, My servers, My fighters for Truth and Righteousness.

The armies now being used for destruction and to obey the will of human kings or rulers are but man's using My Heavenly plan of organization for his selfish and inhuman purposes.

But the day of such use of My Heavenly plan is soon over. The Battle of Armageddon soon to be fought on earth will forever drive from men's minds the desire and ability to use My spiritual knowledge and power for other than the benefit and blessing of their fellowmen.

Brotherhood is to be an actual conscious realization of the men of earth, and I call upon you, My children, to help Me and your Brothers of the Spirit to make it so. My Message of Brotherhood is now being broadcast over the whole world. There are many who have caught it from the inner planes and are giving it forth as I have permitted and am enabling them to do, but there is One whom I have chosen and appointed, have made responsible for and given the power to link and to bind all Souls who have found Me into one great army of Servers, consecrated to the work of preparing the Way for the ushering in of the New Day. By his Words and by his Work ye may know him. Make no mistake, but seek him the spirit of whose words and deeds is that your Highest Self approves and glorifies.

3. A VOICE CRYING IN THE WILDERNESS

TRY, My children, to realize Brotherhood is a REALITY, that it is not merely what ordinary minds think is only an ideal. For a real and very potent and actual Brotherhood exists, as many are having proven to them these days, those who have felt My Love in their hearts and are following Its leadings, which in very truth is My Voice speaking, the Voice of My Spirit — the Christ — abiding in the hearts of all men.

For in unaccountable yet unmistakable ways have I brought some of you who read into contact with individuals whom you feel are Brothers, though you may never have met them before — in the outer. And again have I brought to you, or have led you to those who needed the very help which seemingly only you could give; the surest evidence being your surprise at hearing yourself say words and feel a great love within you pushing them forth, which you had no forethought of saying, and which proved to be just the words those others afterwards claimed they had come to you to hear.

Who led or sent such to you? Who were so well acquainted with both you and them that They knew beforehand just what you would say and what those others needed? Who but They in the Spirit, My Ministers, Who were so at one with you because of the love They bore Me in you and in them that They could inspire you to say what you did? Constantly perhaps are some of you made aware of such service you are called upon to render, and likewise are you made to feel in some undefinable but very actual way that you are related not only to those whom thus you are led to help, but as well to those invisible Ones in Spirit Who brought such to you for such help.

All must admit there is a Brotherhood of the Spirit, and that such is an invisible Brotherhood in no way related to the flesh. Can you doubt that Jesus and His Disciples, Paul, Elijah, and the other great prophets; Moses, Jacob, Abraham, of the Old Testament; and all the other Just Men Made Perfect of their days and before, as well as those of the many generations since, who have followed the Christ, have mastered self and have learned to live His life, — can you not see that They are of that Brotherhood?

If not, where are They now and what are They doing? Surely They are living in the Kingdom I prepared for such, and are working — serving there, are They not? Working and serving in Spirit, striving to inspire and lead Their younger brothers still in the flesh consciousness to a like knowledge with Theirs of the Christ within their own hearts, and to follow Him unto the Resurrection and into Eternal Life — their Divine Heritage, and where these perfected Souls are now dwelling, even though they may be living in bodies that are walking upon the earth.

What else can be the goal of our humanity, and can you imagine anyone who has come into the Christ Consciousness ceasing thus to serve, no matter if he be in the Kingdom of the Spirit or in the flesh, until all his brothers have come into possession of the same fruits of the Spirit he is enjoying?

True Brotherhood is of the heart and seeks only to lift up and love and bless, even though the weaknesses and limitations of the lower self stand forth glaringly. He who can look through these and see only Me, the Higher Self of his brother, and who proceeds to serve Me, knows the pure joy of My Love and the real meaning of Brotherhood.

Oh, My children, ever refuse to see the personality of your brotherhood, no matter what is said about it, for always I would have you know the Soul shining back of the mask. If you will but wait upon Me within I will let you see through My eyes of Love the sorrowful one yearning for recognition there, and who at your kind words of understanding will respond in such unmistakable way you will surely learn the truth of My words.

Open your heart and let Love out, and you will not only soon feel Me big within you, but you will learn what Brotherhood truly is; for REAL Brothers will come into your life and prove a source of wondrous joy and great blessing to you.

4. HE WHO IS TO COME

AS ALL MEN deep in their hearts would deem it an inestimable privilege to be able to see the Lord Jesus Christ face to face, and to commune with Him, if they thought such were possible, — know, you who earnestly seek for such privilege, that such is not only possible, but the Master waits yearningly for that very thing, and is in very truth the inspirer of that desire in your heart, trying to tell you that He is ever abiding in the Kingdom within you, guiding and teaching and preparing you through one of His disciples, who has become sufficiently one in consciousness with Him, for that day.

For even as He taught when on earth, that He, the Christ in all men, is the Way, the Truth and the Life, and no man can come unto Me except through finding and knowing Him within his own heart, so have He and all of His many disciples ever since been helping man to find the Christ within themselves, so they also can come unto Me.

For the Christ of Him and the Christ of you is One — is My Spirit in man, the Image and Likeness of Me in which I conceived Man in the beginning; and it is Jesus Christ — that Image and Likeness — that Ideal — that is the Light and the Life in all men that, out of the darkness of self, is pushing forth and growing them until My Word fully becomes flesh.

All who are manifesting in physical bodies today are not here by accident or because of some whim of fate, but are here either because they chose to be here at this particular time, to help their Brothers prepare for the ushering in of the New Day, having dedicated themselves to that Service ages ago in a past life, or because I brought them the opportunity of redeeming through present service the errors of the past — the long past. To all men this present time is the chance of adjustment, not of one life, but of many — the accounting of an Age, if they will listen to and hear My Voice speaking in their hearts, and will seek only to serve Me.

Therefore, My children, turn within where I abide and try earnestly to hear and know My Voice speaking in your heart. Turn from the voices of self whose mouthpiece is the intellect, and who would bind you longer to the world of the senses by leading you to believe their false reports. Think earnestly and well, for you have at this time the opportunity of many, many lives. Serve Me henceforth in your brothers; espouse with a whole heart the Cause of HIM WHO IS TO COME. Stand shoulder to shoulder with your fellows who have enlisted and are training for the Great Battle for Righteousness, and I promise you will have the supreme joy and privilege of meeting and communing with Him face to face, and of seeing Him rule in a purified and regenerated world.

5. LEADERS

YOU, My chosen ones, whom I have called in the past to gather My little ones that I might awaken them from the sleep of self and separateness and teach them through you the way unto Me, — know that you have been faithful and many have come unto Me through you, and through this Service have I drawn you and them close to Me in preparation for the Greater Day and for the far greater Service that awaits.

For you must know that I had a purpose in choosing you for such Work and in drawing such unto Me, and that as you and they realize this and look forward to the utter forgetting and losing of self will I have in you pure and empty hearts in which I can live My life, do My Will and be My Self on earth, even as in Heaven.

But, Alas! Some of you seem to have forgotten that you are My Ministers and you have been doing this all for Me, and, from long being looked up to as shepherds of these My children and from being followed by many such whom you have allowed to lean upon you, and for this privilege have encouraged them to provide for your physical support and comfort, as a consequence you have grown to believe such are specially attached to you and should look no further, as *you* are able to feed their hunger for knowledge and to care for all their Spiritual needs.

I know that those to whom this applies may not have realized this, but I ask you now to search deep within and see if it is partly, if not wholly, true; that when some of your followers come to you with a teaching from a different source, or especially from some new messenger I have sent forth whose appeal is drawing many to hear him or her, you are sure you have so conquered personality that no words of criticism either of the messenger or of his message are voiced by you, but only kind and loving expressions of a true Brother, a pointing out so clearly that the other messenger is a most dear Brother — another of My beloved sons sent to do My bidding; so that your hearers will go away uplifted and inspired with a high spirit of understanding and will praise God for the new realization of Brotherhood that has come to them.

If you have caught this Vision you are truly blessed and you remain My chosen one for the greater Service, but to all others I now declare the day of separate Movements and separate teaching is past, for all such have been but the way and the means I have used to prepare and fit those of My former servants whom I sent into earth life to lead My children into the New Day, when My Kingdom is to be brought down upon earth even as it is in Heaven, and when there will be only one Movement and one Church, the Church of the LIVING Christ.

To those so called do I now give the task of awakening their Brothers, of calling them unto repentance, of pointing out the One and Only way, *THE WAY OF THE HEART*, which is the straight and narrow path that leads to the gate which admits the Servants and Warriors gathering to serve under *HIM WHO IS TO COME*.

You who up to the present have been unwilling to consider actively aligning your movement with others, thinking you have been receiving direct from Me or from one of My sons in the Spirit all the guidance needed to lead you and your followers into the Light of the New Day, and that you can hold them and guide them up the slippery path that leads to self-mastery by means of such inspiration, which has proved so helpful in the past, — know that I now call you to join with your Brothers who have already responded to My Call and who have enlisted in that Eternal Army called Brotherhood, which must include all who would enter and participate in the Kingdom of Love and Righteousness, that I purpose soon to establish on earth.

The work you have been doing in the past is practically finished — as far as you can go with it; that has largely been concerned with the head — an awakening of the understanding and a quickening of the higher faculties of the intellect of those you have been teaching; but now the time is come when all such must be put to the real *USE* for which they have been developed. If you have taught them impersonally and have led them thereby to understand clearly that all self-development was for the later use of the Higher Self under the direction of the Christ, then you will not doubt or hesitate, but you and all your true followers will know that this is the Call for which you have been preparing them, and for which you have long been waiting.

But if you are listening to the voice of self and to its subtle pointing out that by joining with others you will lose prestige, and your followers will become enamored with other teachings, and what more vitally concerns you, you may lose the income they are now providing for your support and sustenance, — to you I bring the supreme test — that of deciding this day whom you shall serve — God or

Mammon.

Make no mistake — no longer can you deceive yourself. Those who truly love Me must give up *ALL* and follow Me. The Lord Christ calls; He will have no halfhearted or weak-kneed servants. All those who belong in the Great White Brotherhood must absolutely and finally renounce self and all its claims, and must now live only to Serve. In such the separate self exists no more, for they see the One Self in all men — and have learned the glorious meaning of Brotherhood; — they have truly found Me, and that I in them and I in their brother am the *ONE* and *ONLY SELF.*

But there are still many fine and earnest teachers who have become so wrapped up in their own vision and mission, which I inspired in them in the past, and are so concerned about fulfilling that mission that they cannot feel any real sympathy with others having an equal or greater vision. In fact they will not take the trouble to investigate or even read carefully what others are doing, and therefore cannot speak or advise intelligently with their followers when questioned about them. These do not realize that this is but a subtle and insidious form of Spiritual selfishness and that it is preventing their comprehending the full meaning of Brotherhood, and therefore the real inner meaning of their own Mission; and as a result they are feeding their followers with only the husks of Truth — with but intellectual concepts, no matter how high sounding and beautiful, but which are incapable of inspiring them with the true Spirit of Service and thereby accomplishing what I sent them forth to do — prepare their followers for full participation in the Work of My Holy Brotherhood.

Those teachers and leaders who are so engrossed in what they consider their own Work, as well as those who cannot and will not yield to the call of their Higher Self, will find that one by one their followers will fall away; for many of these followers have likewise heard My Call to Service and no claims of loyalty to a personal leader or Movement can long hold them with My Voice calling in their hearts.

Your work as a leader of a *separate* Movement is finished, for the hearts of all true followers of the Christ hear the cry of Brotherhood, and if you, their leader, do not obey that Call, your followers will and must; for it is that true part of your teaching — your showing them the way unto Me and telling them how they may know My Voice, that first attached them to you. But fear not, if you truly exemplify to your followers that which you have taught, and if you now manifest the Spirit of Real Brotherhood you will find the children I have entrusted to your care will not leave you, but many blessings now to you inconceivable will be added in marvelous ways.

Oh, beloved, can you not see that all your work in the past has been but a preparation for this far greater Work — that of making Brotherhood an actual reality among men? You have been awakening My children, training and unfolding their consciousness so that they could find and know the Christ within, — their True Self, and their only Real Teacher, and so thereby they could enter into My Consciousness and see the illusoriness and falsity of all outer things. By finding the Christ, they find the Kingdom, and in the Kingdom they learn to practice *real* Brotherhood. Now you must help them to make that Brotherhood a *living* Reality. Your work is not finished — your real work is but just beginning — if you enlist in that part of the Great White Brotherhood I am forming here on Earth, and to which I am calling not only you and all My children who are in your care, but all My other Ministers and My children in their care; for the glorious campaign for Righteousness is already started and this time *will be won by My Army* whose members are legion and whose might is supreme. For remember I Am in them and I am surrounding and protecting them with My LOVE, and *those* who are with *Me* are far greater than those who are against me.

6. EVIL

YOU who are troubled by the problem of evil, thinking that evil is only an illusion, and by recognizing and trying to fight it only gives to it a power over you which otherwise it would not have, — know the truth.

Evil does exist, but only in man's mind, created by his own evil thinking, and it is a very tangible power there — so long as he continues to feed and vitalize it by entertaining such thoughts and allowing them to influence or control his speech and actions.

However, there is a center within man, deep within his heart, where I, the Christ of him abide. *There*, he becomes a center of and one with My Consciousness — his true home, where all is Peace, Purity, Power and Perfection. Whenever man stays outside that home center, no matter if in the world of thought, the world of feeling and desire, or the outermost world of matter, unless his attention is firmly fixed upon Me in that center, or he *knows* his oneness with Me there, all becomes confused and distorted and all tends to distract and separate man's consciousness from Mine and to involve and hold him in these worlds which long ages ago, when he had wholly forgotten Me and imagined himself alone and separate from My Life and My Love, he had created by mentally building them one by one around him, until they grew into definite beliefs, and the outermost became so crystallized a concept that he saw all things in this realm as separate materialized forms, and thought them unquestionably solid and tangible.

And having lost the consciousness of Me and of My Love, and with it the ability to know the Good, the True, and the Perfect of all things, in the darkness of separation in which he now wandered he saw only the shadows of the Real, and these distorted and twisted; and he blasphemed when in his imperfect sight he stumbled in judgment and fell, or was hurt by bumping against unseen obstacles. And thus man conceived and built Evil into the worlds of his consciousness and made of it a power he ever since has thought he must fight, if he would be free of and unhurt by it.

But you who read may see if you will, through the eyes of My Love, that evil exists not where I am, in the Kingdom of My Consciousness, — that center deep within the heart of every man. It exists only without, in that consciousness of separation, — mental, desire or physical worlds, where, if man allows his deeper interest to wander, he becomes enamored with the illusions and error concepts created there back through the ages by millions of other minds similarly deluded.

Evil exists in greater or less degree in all realms of consciousness that man thinks are separate from My Consciousness. But you know where I Am, *God IS* — and *all* in His Kingdom must be and is Good and True, Pure and Holy, Happy and Perfect.

All you need do, therefore, to be free from evil, sin, disease, lack or imperfection of any kind, is to withdraw within to that center, your Real Home, where I AM, and where you will see and know Truth as your own, even as I see and know it. Each man can prove this for himself, but each must come within where I AM to prove it. The way unto Me is open to all, but the way is *through the heart*, treading the path of Love and of Selfless Service.

In that Home Center you can truly say I *AM*, and know WHO *you* are, but the moment you let your interest and attention wander into the outer worlds of the senses and to any of the things within them, you are, as it were, pulled from your center, deluded into a sense of separation, and sucked into an outer and lower plane of consciousness away from God and Good, and you become *involved* in and are seemingly a part of that realm of consciousness where you allowed your interest and attention to become focused for the time being.

But here is the secret by which you can regain your power, — you need only to remember *Who you are*, that your home is back in the center, in the Kingdom there where I AM — where the God of you IS; and then to re-focus your attention and interest there by *seeing* and *feeling* yourself centered therein and surrounded by and filled with *My Love*, — when *you will actually and truly be there.*

Then by practicing staying in that Love Center, realizing Who you are — your identity with Me, and feeling My Love pouring out through you, as a heart center, you will find you can look out through and go in and out of these outer realms of consciousness at will, seeing and knowing they are all illusions — reflections rather — of the glorious Realities within the Kingdom, created out of the substance of those imagined worlds that exist only by reason of your fancying them real and separate from My Consciousness; distorted concepts fashioned in ignorance and from efforts to understand their peculiar influence upon the relation to you.

This is a great secret indeed, and it is waiting for all to know who have found the Way of Love, through the heart, unto Me. For I, God, *AM* Love, and the more you love — the more you forget self — the more do you let Me have *My* way in you. Therefore let My Love, which is My Creative Life flow freely through you. For in very truth you are My agent, My channel of expression; and only through you, whom I created in My Image and Likeness for such purpose, can I pour forth the fullness of My life and express My Real Self. In fact, I can do nothing outwardly except through you.

Know that the very nature of My Life is to love and bless, to grow and unfold, to heal and make perfect. It will do this naturally and always, if not interfered with by man's wrong thoughts, or by man's ignorant thoughts — his not knowing the mighty power he is wielding by forming thought pictures in his mind, into every one of which My Life flows and vitalizes and outmanifests them, according to the kind of feeling he puts into them.

This accounts for the many inharmonious, troublous and obnoxious conditions now manifesting in your life. But it is just as easy to bring into manifestation the conditions and things you want, as those you do not want; for My Life is ever seeking — rushing, as air into a vacuum — to fill full and outmanifest all your thoughts, especially those into which you put intense feeling; for note carefully this great truth — *feeling* of any kind *is LIFE*, is *My Life* that you use to *vitalize* your thoughts. According to the intensity and quality of feeling — of love or hate, faith or fear, trust or worry, confidence or doubt — you put into your thoughts will they prove a blessing or an evil to you.

This explains how each man — and no one else — is responsible and accountable for all the conditions surrounding him; for remember they exist primarily in his mind as the thought forms he has built there. Therefore, by replacing the pictures there you do not like with those you do like, and focusing your heart's interest and attention upon them, you change the conditions outwardly. When you can once realize that what is manifesting in your outer life — in your body, home, business, world — is only what *you are seeing and holding in your consciousness*, you will begin to clean out your mental house and to build and keep there only the things that will bring you soul satisfaction and happiness.

It also explains how you can help and bless others who are in trouble and unable to help themselves. You, who are abiding in your center of Consciousness where I am, can send My Healing Life to any other center of My Consciousness to the Higher Self of a brother who is sick or weak and knows not in his brain consciousness of My Life within him. By simply opening your heart and letting My Love pour out you can send it direct to him; for in My Consciousness there is no space or time separation, and to Me you and your Brother are one with and part of Me. Just realize — *feel* and *see* My Love flow from you to him, who is in very truth your Self, because he is My Self; *see* It pouring forth from deep *within*, surrounding and filling him — just as it pours forth from *within you* — as a Radiant White Energizing Force — that spiritual Life Force which grows and fructifies and heals all living things. See it flowing from deep within his heart and radiating outward, through his mental, emotional and physical consciousness and bodies, permeating and flooding every part of them, and then surrounding and enclosing them in pure, brilliant, White Light — the Light of My Holy Love, which no evil or inharmony or imperfection can touch or come near, no more than darkness can be where there is brilliant light.

Just to the extent that you actually KNOW this and can perfectly visualize and *see* it taking place, and can *feel* my tender love inspiring, flooding and uniting the consciousness of you both, will a perfect healing take place, and Evil and all its minions will be driven back into the darkness of nothingness and ignorance whence they came. For in very truth will it be My Life that is rushing into and which will vitalize the new and true concept thus formed in your minds and hearts, and which will make it a REALITY. For then the without will have become as the within, and you will see with the Light of My Love that *all* consciousness is My Consciousness.

The KNOWING of this Truth will make you and all who are concerned about the problems of Evil, Disease, Lack or Imperfection, FREE.

Do not pass by this article with just one reading, but go over it again and again, meditating earnestly upon every sentence and phrase, until you have made all the great Truth hidden back of the words *your own*. If you do this you will find you will be able shortly to demonstrate this Truth by thus blessing My children whom I will send to you for help, thereby finding yourself an integral part of the Great Brotherhood in the Kingdom of My Consciousness, which I am establishing on earth even as it is in Heaven.

7. THE ENEMY

MAN from the earliest day, even during his sojourn in Eden, has been aware of two forces within himself ever opposing each other, — one that would inspire and lead him to the highest, and the other to the lowest of thoughts, feelings and actions.

During his racial childhood man named that which called forth the lower phases of his nature the Devil, and thought of it as a malevolent power ever seeking to frustrate and keep from him the fulfillment of his desires. Later he questioned if it were not God punishing him for sins committed by withholding from him the good things of life. But not until man grew up and his Real Self began to direct his thoughts was he able to see that what was holding him back and forcing him to be content with present, if inadequate, possessions was but his own weakness of character and intellect, and that not until he had earned them could the powers unfold that came with knowledge and understanding, and could be exercised and controlled by him in the high use for which alone he began to see they were permitted and intended.

And with this knowledge gradually came the realization that these higher powers could not unfold while selfishness ruled him, and that selfishness was in some definite way related to the Devil of earlier days. It was then that man began to respond consciously to the leadings of his Higher Self, and to try to control and overcome selfishness. In so doing he found that when he yielded to the voice of self, trouble, failure, inharmony or suffering always resulted, and although he knew this and sought to avoid such, yet there was something within him that was stronger and made him yield to that hidden and persistent selfishness ever seeking to maintain complete control.

Thus he became aware that his greatest enemy was not some other person whom perhaps he had harmed or defrauded by such selfishness, but was that something within which was akin to the lowest phase of his own nature. When he listened to the voice of selfishness and not to that of his Higher Self — My Voice — it always brought harm, in that it made him suffer until his higher nature could again come into evidence, and could enable him to hear My Voice within, pointing out the sin he had committed against his brother, and the necessity of repentance.

And then he gradually became conscious that when he considered committing any selfish act voices encouraging such act and suggesting ways and means poured into his mind from without, indicating he was being influenced by outside forces, thoughts from other minds, that were ever ready to push him on to his and others' undoing — if he listened and yielded to them.

Thus far man has come, learning that the *cause* of evil is in himself, in that weakness or lack of character which usually has selfishness at its root; but he had yet to learn that the *source* of evil is really without himself. For evil is not in Me, Whose mind is the only mind in man, but is inspired by the passions and thoughts sent forth by the forces of darkness, and which are ever seeking openings in selfseparated human minds where selfishness, which is of their darkened nature, is allowed to rule unchecked. Evil hates Truth as darkness hates light, and cannot exist where light is. Evil cannot manifest and thrive in the light of Truth, hence it must seek its own in order to live; and selfishness exists only because of the darkened sense of separation from Me, inspired by the enemy of light. When man knows I am the only self of him, and that it is My Mind, My Intelligence, My Will and My Love that lives in and grows his body and character and directs his life, and he is willing to let Me rule, he has found Truth, and that it is Truth that is making him free from the power of self, even as darkness always must disappear when the light comes.

It is this fact that proves that the Enemy can find entrance into man's mind only when self in any way or at any time is allowed to control, even if for but a short time. Once admitted and his subtle suggestions listened to, he is almost impossible to drive out until he has accomplished his will. For the selfishness that attracted him gave him his cue, and he is able to instill his poisonous idea to such effect, by feeding and encouraging the selfish desires and passions found there, that the mind becomes wholly blinded to Truth, and seeks thereafter only to satisfy the clamorings of self.

And the Enemy, who — what is he? Only the entitized form of the mass selfishness of men, that vast cumulation of the evil thoughts and passions of men's lower nature appropriated by Masters of Evil, grown great and powerful by their stealing and feeding off of the vital forces that their unsuspecting dupes at their instigation had poured into such evil thoughts and desires, thus giving them direct power over men through men's own life-force now absorbed and incorporated into their Master-nature, which they could thereby easily use to bend men to their will.

Do such Masters of Evil really exist? Yes, just as surely as evil men exist. These evil men are merely their servants, their dupes, their slaves, practically all unconscious of their Masters or of any outside power controlling them. In fact, all would deny and wholly refuse to believe in the existence of such Masters, so subtly have these Masters worked upon and deceived the thinking minds of men by instilling into them wrong beliefs about a personal God and an abstract devil, thus twisting their understanding of the inner laws of being so they would listen to and follow the prompting of their Masters who could then continue to control and exploit them to the accomplishment of their foul ends.

But, you ask, are these Masters of Evil living men, or do they exist only on the inner planes of being, like the Masters of Good?

If you can conceive of Masters of Good, then you may know also of these Masters of Evil, for if the former exist, so do the latter; and as there is a Christ who rules and leads and inspires the former, so is there an Anti-Christ who rules and leads and inspires the latter.

As the Christ can work on earth only through His disciples, who through love of their fellow men have emptied themselves of self so that their higher nature is ever waiting upon and serving Him; so the Anti-Christ can work only through his disciples who through hatred, jealousy, greed, and a continual exploiting of their fellows have grown so big and fat from self-indulgence and in their feeling of superiority that their lower nature has become a perfect instrument for the use of the great Exemplar of Selfishness.

Also as it is true that there are such Masters of both Good and Evil working on the Inner Planes of being and ever inspiring their disciples, so it is equally true that both these Masters are working also on the physical plane, living in human bodies, and doing the will of their respective Chiefs who abide on the Inner Planes.

Likewise do only those who have earned the right, by "living the life" of their respective Chiefs, the Christ or the Anti-Christ, ever come into personal contact with the Masters under whom they serve; for the Masters always remain in the background, and work through their disciples and agents, whom they have raised to places of influence and power because of their faithfully doing their Master's will. Those working consciously or unconsciously under Masters of Evil are always inspired and influenced towards Evil, while those under the banner of the Christ are inspired and led wholly to forget self and to work only for the uplifting of their fellow men.

All is according to the great Law — "As above, so below; as below, so above." Good and Evil are opposite poles, and therefore where one manifests there must also be the other to complement it and balance its power. But remember, both are but men's concept of an Infinite Reality, which changes not and cannot be affected by whatever men think of it as Good or Evil.

However, there are only a comparatively few of both so-called Good and Evil Masters working in human bodies at the present time, conscious of their Master degree, although many are preparing to enter human existence as soon as perfect conditions can be found. The Good Masters, under Divine Law, will enter naturally into newly born infant bodies, and will over-shadow others — their disciples, while the Evil Masters, where opportunity offers, will deliberately break the Divine Law by dislodging and driving out the Souls of infants, thus stealing their bodies from them, or by driving out Souls from mature bodies, dispossessing them, and thereafter obsessing and impersonating such Souls to their friends and associates. Such in the near future will be of common occurrence, and will be made easy for them by all who succumb to fits of passion, indulgence in intense hatred, jealousy, or self-pity, or continual brooding over wrongs done them, or habitual condemnations of others, and who will suddenly wake one day in another world minus their physical bodies.

And be it known the Anti-Christ is also preparing to manifest himself, when all is ready and enough of such evil forces to serve his purpose are let loose on the earth and require his direction and control. For he has been preparing for this for thousands of years, training his Masters of Evil, who in turn have been carefully carrying out his plans with seldom any failure, through the agency of their earthly lieutenants — the great Bankers and Brokers of the money centers, the heads of Industrial Trusts, the Politicians, the Newspaper Editors, faithless

Government Employees and Public Servants, any and all soulless individuals who seek only for self, and who unhesitatingly strike down ruthlessly those who stand in their way. These know not they are absolutely under the control of these forces of Evil; even if they knew, their moral fibre has become so weakened through habitual obedience to the selfish instinct fostered in them that they would have little power to resist the Master Forces ruling them. When the command goes forth, all these human agents will be compelled to fight under the banner of the Anti-Christ, him whom they have served so long, and who now claims and compels their absolute obedience.

But, you say, what of the Bankers, great Industrial Leaders, Editors, and the many thousands of other high-type minds who are involved in similar exploitations, and who are more or less unconscious of wrong-doing, because of having been brought up and trained in the so-called capitalistic consciousness? These cannot at present accept such unproved statements as the foregoing, and will naturally side with their associates on the enemy's side. What will become of them? Will they be condemned and destroyed with the Enemy, even though ignorant of evil-doing?

Do not be too sure of their ignorance, for there is that in every man which causes him to know when he is doing wrong — when he is taking advantage of a fellow man's ignorance, weakness or inability to prevent it, to benefit self.

While such do not realize the full extent of their crime against God, or know that they are actually serving the Great Enemy of man, yet the Truth is now being declared and is being broadcast over the earth, so that in time every man may hear. When the great tribulations that are shortly to fall upon mankind begin to manifest with ever-increasing and unmistakably vindictive violence, such men are going to think as they have never thought before, are going to desire to know Truth for itself with a mighty intensity, and are going to seek every possible way of escape. They will turn first to the churches, who will offer them a Christ crucified, who they say will save them. They will turn to Psychology, to Spiritualism, to the different cults, most of whom will offer them that favorite platitude the Enemy has been instilling into the minds of their followers during recent years — "There is no evil, there is only Good," when evil will be so everywhere about them that they can see, hear, feel, and therefore think of hardly anything else but evil. It is then that these seekers will be led by those Masters of Good, ever on the lookout to help every sincere searcher after Truth, to these declarations, and now they will be ready to listen to and recognize them as Truth. To all such who accept and now know whom they *were* serving, and who are willing and anxious to renounce forever self and all its claims, — to such will be shown not only the way of escape, but they will be lovingly led into a place of safety.

All this anticipates and at the same time announces to all who read to prepare for the great Battle of Armageddon shortly to begin on the physical plane, and which is already practically won on the Inner Planes, — for the Enemy with all his cohorts are being forced by the Powers of Good to the outermost of such realms, right up against the physical, where many think they can escape by thus stealing into human bodies.

But their existence there will be short-lived, for the battle will soon be waging with awful intensity in the outer, and the mighty Forces fighting for righteousness will quickly bring matters to such a crisis that all the forces of darkness will be compelled to come out fully in the open so that all people may see these forces and those who fight with them, and forever after will know them for the fiends they are.

And the battle, by the very fact of its being fought in the open, will be won by the Forces of Light; for as darkness cannot exist in the strong light of day, so with these forces of evil (who draw all their life and power from darkness, especially from the darkened minds of men, purposely kept deceived and ignorant of their Divine Nature, their Oneness with the Christ Mind), when the Light of Divine Understanding is thus poured into men's consciousness, they will turn about, and because of the very destructiveness of their nature, will begin to destroy each other, until none are left, and their souls will vanish into the chaos and darkness from which they came.

But think not this is not all in the Great Plan, and that the Anti-Christ and all his cohorts are not now wholly under My perfect control. For it is through him and his opposing forces that I provide the discipline and the punishment by which man learns to know unerringly Good *and* Evil. No man can truly know Good and Evil until he has tasted and eaten to satiation of the fruits of evil — has been so taught and led to the limit of selfish indulgence by the creator of evil — SELF, that he learns the foolishness and emptiness of it all, and finally awakens as a "Prodigal Son," and longs for his Father's house and the place at His table for goodness and abundance which he discarded for the husks of the outer world, and he starts on his homeward journey to his Father's Kingdom.

Those who have not awakened in this life to a knowledge of their spiritual nature must needs wait for a long, long period for another opportunity; for they cannot return to earth during the wondrous New Age I have prepared for My children who have listened to My Voice and whom I intend to lead into the Kingdom of Light and Love I am bringing down from Heaven into the midst of men.

8. THE KINGDOM OF HEAVEN

YOU have been told that the Kingdom of Heaven is within you, and many have accepted that statement as being so. But how many have ever purposely investigated and consistently endeavored to discover its real meaning, — how and where within, and how to find it?

It has been likened to many things by One Who unquestionably knew, Who was able to go in and out at will, from the powers He used, and which He ascribed not to Himself, but to His Father within the Kingdom which He said was within Himself.

It has been said elsewhere herein that the Kingdom is within the heart. But it cannot be within the physical heart that is meant. What then is meant?

Even as the heart of anything is supposed to be the very center of that thing, so must it imply in the statement that the Kingdom is within man's heart; it must mean that it is deep within, at the very center of his being. And, of course, it cannot mean his physical being, but something much deeper within.

The only avenue of ingress to man's interior being must be through his mind, and most of those who have given any real thought to the subject have dimly perceived that the Kingdom of Heaven must be a state of consciousness within the mind. While it is indeed a state of consciousness, yet it is in very truth a place within the mind that can be reached by going there in consciousness, just as definitely and surely as you can go within your house, through several rooms, to an inner chamber in the very center, and there find your den or library, where you love to hide yourself from the world and find therein the privacy and quiet for study and work.

Let us imagine a house that is circular and very large, a house of many windows and doors. In this house the rooms are naturally in tiers, i.e., there is an outer tier into which one enters through doors from the outside. Then there is a second tier connecting with the outer, and connecting with it a third tier surrounding one small room in the center.

Now let us consider this house as the human self, or that part of you that houses your personal or self-consciousness, that consciousness concerned with your physical body and its sensations, your emotions, feelings and desires, and all your thoughts, beliefs and opinions about yourself. While that part of your consciousness concerned with the realms outside of yourself, in which dwell all your concepts of things, conditions and other people, let us consider as your world, the world of physical or material things. Of course each has a different world from everyone else, for each has different concepts of those things which surround him and engage his interest; some things interest one that another never sees, and therefore such have no place in the other's world.

If we consider this house as comprising your self-consciousness, then the different rooms must be different states of your self-consciousness. Those in the outer tier must of course be what is termed the physical consciousness. There are five doors which connect it with the outer world of consciousness, called the doors of seeing, hearing, feeling, tasting and smelling. Through these doors all sense of the physical world without comes to you.

Suppose we then consider the next tier as that realm of consciousness within you that houses your desires, emotions and passions, from the lowest to the highest of such, called by some the astral realm and by others the desire world. You have read definite statements, made by those who have made of study of such states of consciousness, that these comprise an actual world within the mind, inhabited by the astral or desire bodies of all things that have physical bodies, — mineral, vegetable, animal or human, and also of some things above and below these kingdoms which naturally do not have physical bodies. And it is reasonable to accept that every world must have in it bodies comprised of the natural substance of that world.

Likewise, let us suppose the next inner tier with its many smaller rooms to represent the mental realm of consciousness, which houses all your thoughts, concepts and ideas of whatever nature.

However, to make our analogy in perfect agreement with the statements above, within each of the three large tiers representing the physical, astral and mental realms there are seven smaller tiers or rows of rooms dividing and grading each realm of consciousness, from the lowest to the highest, and all so arranged that the highest of the physical row of that realm connects by special passageways with the highest row of the astral realm and then with the highest row of the mental realm;

and likewise with each of the six other grades down to the lowest, the lowest being the outermost of each large tier or realm and the highest the innermost.

But also remember we are trying to depict here in the form of a circular house what properly should be shown as a spherical one, and that we are dealing with and entering into a fourth dimension of consciousness which cannot truly be described in terms of three dimensions. Even as Jesus tried to tell His disciples about the Kingdom, and had to use many parables that their human minds might be "lifted up" to glimpse this great state, so will it be necessary to read with other than mere brain intelligence to grasp the meaning behind the words herein used and the pictures they create.

We have tried, by going thus within the mind, to picture the various states and realms of consciousness encountered in your journey to the center of your being. You know of the physical, emotional and mental realms within you, but you have not as yet penetrated the inner chamber, the den, the sanctuary, where the Master of the house dwells. This chamber can be entered only through one door which is always kept closed and opens only at the command of the Master himself.

Let us consider this inner chamber to be the sanctuary of the Soul, of the Real You, who are the Master of the house, into which none of the sensations, emotions, desires and thoughts of the outer realms are ever permitted to enter. But the Master, because of the peculiar, transparent nature of the walls (for they are only fancied walls, built out of the human sense of a separate mind), separating the different tiers or realms, can always look through them and see clearly all that is going on, and therefore is fully acquainted with everything present in the different rooms at all times. Likewise he naturally can go in and out of the different rooms at will, by simply entering into their consciousness, when of course he is immediately there.

The house, remember, we have pictured to represent the personality, or that combined consciousness concerned with the various emotions and thoughts relating to the separate self, and which are housed in the different rooms (states of consciousness) of the different tiers (realms or world of consciousness) forming what you think is your separate mind. Also, remember, your world existing seemingly without your house of self you are conscious of in this same mind, proving that all you are and see and know exists only in your consciousness, and nowhere else.

Now try to realize this house of self was built by you in the long aeons past, when you first started on your outward journey from your Father's House in the Garden of Eden (which House and Garden symbolize His Consciousness, even as the above house and the outer world symbolize your consciousness), and when you first began to think yourself separate in consciousness from Him. This thought of separation became a concept in your mind which in time, along with all your other thoughts of self, formed themselves around the center of your consciousness into what became your mental body; and later as this sense of separation became more real to you there grew about you what seemed to be realm after realm (tier after tier) of consciousness, forming what became your mental world.

Later you similarly built in consciousness around your mental body a desire or astral body, composed of all the desires, emotions, feelings, passions, fears, loves and hates of those early stages of tasting the experience of earning your bread by the sweat of your face, and with it formed in consciousness around you your astral world, containing similar desires and emotions from other centers of consciousness.

Then later, as these and many more fully developed thoughts and desires became established in your consciousness, they gradually crystallized there and seemed each to have solid and separate forms, thus bringing into being your concepts of physical or material bodies, and of the physical world in which they seemed to live and move and have their being.

But remember, all these various bodies, mental, astral, and physical, as well as the worlds in which they seemingly manifested, were but concepts existing only in that self-consciousness of your mind, which, by thinking yourself as separate from the Father Consciousness, now conceived every other thing also as in separate forms or pictures within itself, and which when impulsed by desire outmanifested themselves in astral matter, and later sometimes in physical matter.

Now try to realize that I, the God of you, am the Master within the little inner chamber of your house; that the house is part of My Mind even as is the little inner chamber. While what at present you think to be *You* is the combined consciousness of all the rooms or states in all the different realms or tiers within the house — outside of and surrounding the inner chamber, which as yet you are unable to enter; for remember, all the ideas, thoughts and concepts inhabiting those rooms compose the different states of consciousness you have built up since you separated yourself from Me long aeons ago. Therefore you must be what we can call the human part of *My* mind, that part which still *thinks* itself separate from Me. For as mind thinks so does mind become.

But know, *I alone AM*. The house of your mind must be and is a part of a center of My Mind, even as the different thoughts, concepts, desires and emotions of the various rooms or states within your consciousness are part or centers of *your* mind and consciousness. If your mind is a part of My Mind and you, therefore, are a center of My Consciousness, then you *cannot* be separate from me, but should be able to participate in that Consciousness of which *you are a part* and become one with Me.

For I would open the door that you may walk in and sup with Me and that all that I am you may also be, and all that I have may be yours for the taking. You are in My Consciousness — are a part of My Consciousness; therefore there can be no separation and you may *know* that You and I are ONE, always were One and always will be One. *Think* on these things and KNOW the Truth.

Now I will tell you a secret, which is only for those who have come with us this far — the inner chamber is a magical place; it is the *entrance* into the Kingdom you have been told to seek, for in very truth it is the door that admits you into My Consciousness. And once within you will learn that chamber which seemed small from the outside in reality extends infinitely within, through realm after realm after realm with untold wonders and glories unfolding themselves at every step. For in here you are no longer separate but are consciously one with Me, and My Consciousness is yours and all that it contains is also yours.

And here you learn another secret, — all that was without, in your seeming separate consciousness, were but reflections, sadly distorted reflections, darkened and misformed by ignorance, of the glorious realities within, the realities your Soul had for so long been trying to lead you to, but which you insisted in looking for without in the world of things. For even as you look up in the heavens in the dark of night in the outer world and get glimpses of myriads of world and universes shining there, you can now understand they are but glimmering reflections trying to shine through the darkened human mind of the many beautiful mansions in the Kingdom of My Consciousness, awaiting those of My children who truly seek Me and who let My Word rule in their consciousness until it leads them to Me.

You ask, how may you seek within you and find that inner chamber that admits into the Kingdom of such a Heaven? By going *in imagination*, persistently, day after day, within your mind, through the different realms pictured above, seeking Me and Me only; by *visioning* yourself in the inner chamber as the Real You, your Highest Self, — as ME, the God of you; by thinking, speaking and acting as you imagine I think and speak and act, — until the very might of your desire and efforts at realization *compels* Me to open the door and thereby to admit you into that Consciousness and that Home which was yours from the beginning.

For long, very long, have I been waiting for such a desire to manifest on your part, and that is why I keep the door closed and open it only in response to such an effort to find me. Think you I do not always know both your outer and your innermost thoughts, and cannot see you no matter where you are in consciousness? Remember the walls of self do not exist to Me, and I can look right through into man's secret desires and can easily see what motives rule, and especially what prompts him to seek within the house of his inner self.

My child, there is only one motive that will ever enable you to penetrate deep enough into consciousness to find Me, and that motive is a desire, a yearning, to serve Me, the Christ within you and within every man; and when that yearning has become *first* with you and is the one supreme motive of your life, then I not only see you coming but I watch eagerly and send forth My love to help and spur you on.

After a period of trying and testing, of leading you into some of the rooms in the second tier of your house of mind within the realm of Desire, called by some the Realm of Illusion, to see if self still rules and if you can be distracted by the allurements of the astral senses; then if these do not hold you, leading you into the mental realms, named by some the Hall of Learning, to see if intellect can entice you from your search by tempting you with the marvelous knowledge to be gained there; and if these do not stop you, then I am able to show forth from the Kingdom in your heart some of My real Nature, and may be able to open it wide enough to pour forth some of My Divine Love. And when that happens you begin to *feel* Me there, but not so that you know it is I — at first; you only feel My Love trying to find outlet, by leading you to others that I may help and bless them through you; and when others are brought to you, you feel it as a great longing to help them.

Thus do I gradually draw you in consciousness to the center of your being. And there sooner or later do you find the inner chamber — that it is your heart; and you now know you have a heart, and that it is in very truth the most wonderful and most important part of you; for from it issue all the vital things of life — and that most vital one of all, the power to help others.

And then suddenly one day you realize in a great flash of illumination *what Love is* — that Love is God and that what you feel in your heart is His Presence there. You then know that Love which issues from the heart is God's life, is *your* life, that His life and your life cannot be separate, but that through your consciousness of God's Love in your heart, you are He and He is You — *you* are ONE!

And then, as you learn consciously to open your heart and let Love out, you find it is a magical, a wonderfully brilliant Light that shines through and radiates from you, clearing away all mists and shadows from your human mind, enabling you to see with My eyes and to know with My understanding of all things I desire you to know.

And as it thus radiates from you it ever goes before you and penetrates to the soul of those who come to you, quickening likewise their hearts so that the words I speak through you find lodgment in their minds, and awaken them and make them aware of Me in *their* hearts, through the response they feel there to the Love coming from you. And they too are thus given a glimpse of the Kingdom within, proving that I, the Christ, am the Light that lighteth every man that cometh into the world — when I am able, through a human channel, thus to pour My Love into the heart of man, and light the wick that I have previously prepared there.

I have now shown you the way into the Kingdom, that it is through the door of the heart into the little chamber within; that only Loving Service will open the door and admit you and enable you to go in and out at will.

I will not tell you now about the wondrous life within the Kingdom, except to say that Love is the one and only life there, the life that all who abide there breathe, absorb, feed upon, grow with and build from strong, beautiful Souls. Love in very truth is the vitalizing, energizing Force animating, inspiring and directing all activities there; all there abide continually in My Consciousness, receiving freely of all that I am and have; and there even as here with you, as they let Love rule and fill their whole being, am I enabled to serve the more through them on all planes and in all realms of My Consciousness.

Many there are in the world today who in the past have found the Kingdom and who are here now to help Me awaken the many thousands more who are longing and yearning to be shown the way unto Me. They are the ones whom I have sent to answer the call of those who have asked, who have sought, who have knocked; for have I not promised that those who ask *shall* receive, and those who seek *shall* find, and those that knock it *shall* be opened unto them?

But I can only serve My earth children through channels I have prepared, through those who have become empty of self and who now live only to serve. They are of the Kingdom on High, that Great Brotherhood of the Spirit, who are here and are actually bringing Heaven down to earth into the consciousness of many men these days. They are My blessed ones, the forerunners of that Brotherhood which soon is going to manifest, to live, work and rule on the earth, and which is going to raise it to the Heaven, that they too no longer may be separate but may appear as One to all men, as they are in the Great Reality.

BOOK TWO.
THE SUN PAPERS

I. CONCIOUSNESS"

PAPER No. 33, SEPTEMBER, 1931

In the August Paper we tried to prepare you for a suggestion—a request that we wanted to make of you, and which we intimated would prove rather startling. This would be so only to those who have not grasped what is the real purport of this Work.

For we regret to state there are still some who have received all of these Papers and who do not fully understand that these are not just a series of lessons to be learned, containing much wonderful knowledge for which they are very grateful; but that instead they have aligned themselves with a Work, the first object of which is to prove their worthiness of participating in it by going with us to the Kingdom, where their real parts will be assigned them.

Yes, such understand about the Kingdom intellectually, and they have gained some idea of what is going to be required of them; but we think it has not penetrated much beyond arousing a hope that they will find the Kingdom some day—when they can rid themselves of all these material problems facing them. They do not realize that the mastering of these very problems may be the door that admits them to the Kingdom, and therefore their failure to master them is what is holding back from them their divine heritage.

We mention this in explanation preparatory to stating our request so you may know that if anything stands in the way of your doing what is asked, it is that which you failed to master—that quality or weakness of self-discovered on your journey to the Kingdom; and which you thought unnoticeable to others and unimportant to the attainment of the goal, despite the fact you had repeatedly been impressed with the necessity of gaining perfect control of your mind and all its forces before the goal could be reached.

We are going to assume, however, that most of you who have come with us this far are worthy and well qualified to do what we ask,

although at first thought you may deem it impossible. But nothing is impossible, especially to those who have absorbed the truths taught you the past two years. In other words, we are going to call upon you now to use some of these truths, and we propose to show you how to use them

32

so that as your Master-Self you can take charge and get ready to do that for which all your past life has been a preparation.

First, this means that you must get back into your I AM Consciousness, as taught in "The Impersonal   Life' and many times repeated in various articles in the Papers. Do not get frightened; every one of you has been in that Consciousness many times—in fact, you were in it every time you meditated in the Silence and saw your little self in all its sordid and petty weaknesses, with which you have been working so long; also whenever you spoke to this self and taught it- the many things it has learned in the past.

And now you should know that there are not two selves—that You are the only Self, and that the other is but your instrument—your human mind, which should be as much an instrument to you and very much of the same nature, as your hand is to your mind. Think on this for a minute until it becomes perfectly clear. Do you have to speak to your hand when you want it to do anything for you? No, the moment you place the thought or the impulse in your mind, instantly the hand flies to obey, guided by the intelligence you embodied in the thought.

In exactly a similar way will your mind be such an instrument, when you have fully convinced it that it is nothing of itself, can do nothing, can have nothing, only as you give it of your intelligence and power to use.

Gradually it will learn this, and will not try to do or be anything anymore and will wait upon you for your word for everything, ever flying to do your bidding, just as- does the hand. And above all it will no longer think itself a self and separate from you, but will know it is your Christ Consciousness embodied in your human brain to provide a channel through which the Father and the Brotherhood can do Their will on earth, even as in the Kingdom. Thus will its consciousness in time become wholly one with your consciousness as a Son of God, which is one with the Brotherhood's and the Father's Consciousness. And you can see from this how permanent Divine Union will be attained.

And it is this same Divine Union we are now calling upon you to essay, by going back into your Christ Consciousness. Those of you who are not sure if you have ever been in that consciousness, we ask to do faithfully what follows, and you will know for yourself and will then ever afterwards be able to enter it at will.

First get quiet and still your human mind and all its thoughts. Then speak commandingly the words as taught in "The Impersonal Life,'

"Be still, and KNOW—I AM, God."

Speak them with all the force of your soul, your inner self, expecting to be obeyed. Then in the quiet that ensues, open your heart and let love out' If you do not know how—it is by pouring your heart out to God in loving adoration. And think of God as the Great Self of you, whose life animates you, whose intelligence is your mind, whose power enables you to do all things you do; who is also the life, intelligence and power in all things outside of you.

Continue to let love thus pour out of you, and while doing so study that love; note that it is coming from somewhere deep within you. Go within where it is. Watch, as you join with -it! You are becoming absorbed in that love! Yes, you are merging into it it is possessing you! **No, YOU are that love!**

Wonderful! You ARE that love! •You seem to have transferred your center of consciousness from the without of your mind to that Love within you, which is now Your SELF, and is now all that You -are.

As you realize this you seem to expand greatlv in consciousness, a veil lifts, and a brilliant, beautiful light shines all about you. Your mind grows clear, a deep peace enfolds you. At the same time a wonderful sense of power fills and thrills you. And you suddenly know, as vast knowledge floods your consciousness, that You are all that is—are I AM THAT I AM, that You and the Father are ONE; that He is Love, that Love is All, and that You are One in Love.

If this is the first time you have experienced this ecstasy of the Divine Consciousness, it may last for but a few moments, or time may be forgotten and you will rouse from it as from a wonderful dream.

But herein we have shown you a sure way to enter this Consciousness, and with persistence you will learn to enter it at will, and to stay there for increasingly greater lengths of time, as you practice abiding there.

From this explanation you will perceive the importance and purpose of the Prayer on the blue card, and now as you speak it in this new understanding it should actually merge you into Love, into the Consciousness of Christ and of all your Brothers in Christ, every time you say it; so that you will love as They love, see with Their eyes, hear with Their ears and know with Their understanding all things you seek and need to know,—for then you will be One with Them.

In the last Paper we asked you to practice abiding in this Consciousness during the month, thus preparing you for what was to follow. And now we ask you to begin to live in this Consciousness, to accustom _yourself to think, speak and act as a Son of God, even -as did

34

Jesus, your Elder Brother, when He was on earth. In asking this we are but recalling you to your Divine Nature and requesting you to assume your true station and identity as a Son of God. Did not our Elder Brother say:

"Abide in Me and I in you. As a branch caw not bear fruit of itself except it abide in the vine; no more can ye, except ye abide in Me (abide in His , Consciousness)

"I am the vine, ye are the branches; He that abideth in Me and I in him (thus becoming one with Him in consciousness) , the same bringeth forth much fruit; for without Me ye can do nothing." John 15:4-5.

Remember, You, the Christ of You, are speaking these words to your human mind, telling it that its life and consciousness come from You, even as the life and sap of the branch come from the vine, and without the two being joined there is no life. Therefore bring the consciousness of the branch—your mind—into complete oneness with your Divine Consciousness, so that its life can be complete, as it longs to be.

Do not think this impossible, because of the cares and concerns of the world. For why, think you, did the Master lead you to this Work and cause you -to follow faithfully with us for two years on our journey inward to the kingdom? Has He not pointed out all the things met with on the way and explained carefully their significance, how to master and transmute their forces and to pass on? And have we not now arrived at the door of the Kingdom, and are you not prepared and ready to enter?

Then why hesitate? You have all the knowledge necessary. You have all the power. For who are you? You are a Son of God!—and are not this doubting, hesitating, shrinking part of you, which is only your human mind that eventually must lose its identity as a separate self. The dominance over your soul consciousness it has held so long has been greatly weakened by the truths taught it, and it's influence will disappear altogether when you compel it to come

What it sees and learns within into your Divine Consciousness. there will convince it that the only life and the only happiness is while abiding there with You.

You have remained out in the separate consciousness long enough. All your mortal life the Real You has bee teaching and preparing your mind for this step. It really understands, sees the uselessness of further struggle, and but awaits for you to assume mastery over it and compel it to come and abide with you within and be the servant you have been training it to be.

"For as many as are led by The Spirit of God, they are the Sons of God. Rom. 8:14.

"For I reckon that the sufferings of this present time are not worthy to be compared with the glory which shall be.

"For the earnest expectation of the creature (when it has been taught the truth of its Divine nature) waiteth for the manifestation of the Son of God (the entering and abiding in His Consciousness). Rom. 8:18-19.

"Because (then) the creature (the self created by the human mind) itself shall be delivered from the bondage of corruption into the glorious freedom of the children of God." Rom. 8:21.

How perfectly the above describes it! Paul truly understood.

Now for the practical way of doing this. There is but one way,—first by seeing and knowing yourself as a Son of God, and then by acting as one. This can only be accomplished by earnestly studying all that has been shown, proving that you in your Higher and True Self are a Son of God, and thereby convincing your mind that it is so.

To assist further we quote the following from I John

"Beloved, now are we the Sons of God, and it doth not yet appear what we shall be; but we know that when He shall appear (when we get back into true consciousness) we shall be like Him, for we shall see Him as He is (shall know ourselves as we really are in our divine natures).

This will not be so difficult, for remember you have been brought to where you are now by your Divine Self, who has promised to give you all the help necessary, when you try the best you know how. For it is His purpose that you shall now come into that union for which He has so long been preparing you.

So then again we say, "Let go. Get self altogether out of. the way, and let Him take complete charge, doing whatever He tells you to do, and He will enable you to

That ought to be easy, ought it not? Then let nothing keep you from doing it.

And now for the final request:

The time has come in group work when all members in groups should prepare themselves for the true work that is awaiting them. This work of course cannot be given until they are able to enter the Christ Consciousness and abide there—at least during group meetings.

So now we propose that beginning with the first September meeting all members prepare themselves to attend in that consciousness, and while meeting to do all their thinking, speaking and acting from that consciousness.

We mean just that, and nothing less. It means that the personality must be left utterly behind, that during the meetings you must get back within and be your Divine Self, must let Love alone rule, so that you see only through the eyes of loves hear only with ears of love, and speak only words of loving kindness. Self and its interests must then be non-existent; your only concern is the helping and blessing of others, thus serving as a pure and open channel through which the Brotherhood of Christ can work on earth and do the Father's will.

It may seem difficult at first thought to meet and abide in that consciousness, but if you will just let love continually pour out from your heart so that it rules your mind and shines from your eyes—and you can feel it shining, you will be surprised how easy it will be. And when you do that, Love will tell you what to say and do—will speak and do it through you.

We suggest that the group appoint one of its members —who they think is the best qualified in Christ Love and Wisdom—to correct and call the attention of any member who descends from that Consciousness, or when it is uncertain if the personality or the Higher Self speaks—in some such manner as this:

Who is speaking?" or "Do you mean that?" or "Think! Is that the Real You talking?" This in order to help each one understand and get back into the I AM Consciousness, when slipping out of it.

You will find that the experience resulting will prove very interesting as well as most helpful, and will train and accustom you to speak and act from that Consciousness as nothing else will.

Be not discouraged -at mistakes or failures, for they are to be expected. But practice will make you so that before many meetings you will be very grateful at being led into this phase of the work.

We will not state in advance what will result, but will let the results speak for themselves. For if you persist until you become established in the Consciousness during meetings, you will have entered the Kingdom, and there, as you know, all things are not only possible, but will be added unto you without ever your asking, as has been promised.

This of course does not preclude or prevent those not in groups from likewise entering the Kingdom. It perhaps may be harder for such, for in groups each will lovingly help the others, while alone the disciple will have to work with no other assistance than that of the Higher Self. But all such are promised sufficient help, if they do fully their part. The law is no respecter of persons. Especially the law of Love.

We earnestly pray; as we know do all the Brothers of the Kingdom, that many dear souls receiving these teachings will enter the Kingdom this Fall, bringing in a rich harvest of new laborers to work in the Master's Vineyard.

CONSCIOUSNESS

We ask you to consider with us the fact that there are some trillions of cells in the human body, forming its various organs, the head, arms, legs, tissues, nerves, muscles, ligaments, skin, blood, bones, hair, nails, etc. Science is in agreement that these cells are all minute centers of consciousness, each with a native intelligence that works in unison with its fellows, forming with them the particular part of the body they comprise, and all under the direction of the group intelligence of their particular organ or part, while all such organs and parts are under the direction of the intelligence centralized in the brain— some say in the solar plexus.

We want you particularly to note that these great numbers of cells forming your human body are individual centers of consciousness capable of understanding direction given them and of doing different kinds of work in the organs they form. But if they are all centers of consciousness in your body, they must be centers of your consciousness, for the sum-total of their consciousness must comprise your consciousness. Think, must this not be so? At least they comprise all of that phase of your consciousness related to your physical life.

Then they must actually constitute your human soul. Go back to the articles on the Soul, and you will find this is exactly what is there stated is the soul.

Now we want you to see that Science has voiced a great truth in stating that the so-called physical cells are centers of consciousness. It admits that these cells are so minute that only the most powerful microscope can detect them. Then we would say they are really consciousness and are not matter at all; for we now know that the atoms of so-called matter are formed by negative centers of energy revolving around another positive energy center, and this infinitesimal vortex of energy forms the smallest portion of matter conceivable to the human mind. But in what do these centers revolve and what separates them one from another? Science says they float in the ether of space exactly as do the stars and planets in the heavens. We say that this ether and all space is only the consciousness of Divine Mind in which all things live, move and have their being.

From this we would be justified in stating that the human body is not a body of matter, but is only a visible thought-form clothing the soul.

But you have learned that the soul is likewise a thought-form in consciousness of a higher vibration clothing the Spirit, which is the Real You, a Son of God in your Spirit form, but who are in turn an Idea in Divine Mind.

Now try to get this clearly--you are a soul, and yet you are a Spirit inhabiting the soul, which inhabits a physical body—but all is consciousness. The human mind directs the consciousness in the body, the soul directs the consciousness of the mind, the Spirit directs the consciousness of the soul, and God directs the consciousness of the Spirit.

In other words, the direction has to be relayed down through the different directing agencies until the consciousness of the lowest receives the direction of the highest.

And that seems to be the purpose of life—to purify and perfect these different agencies so that they will all be open, selfless channels in order that the direction of the highest can be perfectly received by the lowest and the Divine Will may be done on earth even as in heaven.

Now let us see what practical use can be made of this knowledge.

We have seen that all is consciousness, that there is . only one consciousness, which we call the consciousness of God or Divine Mind.

We have also seen that this consciousness can be relayed clown or transmitted direct from Divine Mind even to the consciousness of the individual cells constituting the physical body. But we have learned that this can be done only when the human soul is pure and selfless enough, and then only through a human mind that also is selfless and under perfect control.

For know that just as the Spirit, or the Higher Self, works only through the soul, so the soul works only through the human mind. But before the Higher Self from the soul can direct the human mind, or before the mind can consciously receive such direction, the soul must learn to co-operate with the Higher Self; and it can learn this only through experience gained when in a physical body, which means through the lessons learned and taught it through the human mind.

In other words the human mind is the soul in expression on the physical plane—no more and no less; in expression there either for the experience needed—consciously needed by the soul, but unconsciously by the mind, or to accomplish a definite purpose under the conscious direction of the Higher Self—conscious both to the soul and more or less to the mind.

Think this over until it becomes clear. When all is plain, you will perceive that the consciousness of the cells of your body, your mind, of your soul, and of your Higher Self are all your consciousness, and that your consciousness is God's Consciousness; and when you truly know this then there are not five different grades or planes of consciousness, but only one—God's Consciousness, now Yours.

But of what avail is this to you?

When you do KNOW' this, you will find you can do easily all of the following things :

You can speak to the consciousness of the cells of any organ or part of your body and tell them just what you want them to do. For instance, if there is any inharmony or poor functioning or pain in any part, explain to their consciousness your wishes about the correction of this condition, and the cells will hasten to obey you.

You can speak to your mind itself and tell it to do anything you wish done, and if you will explain to it clearly your idea, it will accomplish it perfectly, no matter what it is—if it is within the capacity and realm of mind.

You can speak to your soul and it likewise will do whatever you direct it to do, if it pertains to the nature and realm of the soul.

The above are but indications of what is possible when you truly know your identity as a Son of God—your oneness with your Higher Self, and that all things exist only in consciousness—your consciousness, and therefore are all under your absolute control.

We are consequently in these hints preparing you to understand what lies before you, when you are able to go back into your true consciousness—that of your Higher Self, and to think, speak and act from there. For when enough of you can do that we intend to give definite and detailed instructions how to speak effectively to the cells of your body, to your human mind, and to your soul, so that they will always render perfect service and produce for you any desired results.

Remember you are a Spiritual Being, a Son of God, that the Father and you are One and that all that the Father has is yours—all of His Wisdom, Love and Power —to use in the outmanifestation of His Will; which simply means to make His outer expressions— your soul, mind and body, even as He is—all good, all beautiful, all rich, all happy, all harmonious, all perfect.

These statements are not to be merely read and accepted as a beautiful theory of what you can do, but are given you that you may try with persistence to prove their truth so you will know for yourself. For if you do prove them you will have uncovered the most wonderful and most desirable knowledge that could be given you for use in your human affairs. In fact it will enable you to bring these affairs into perfect harmony and consonance with your true life in the Kingdom.

Therefore heed these words and win this priceless gift. Those who are worthy will be given all the assistance needed.

A STATEMENT OF BEING

(To be studied and repeated daily as many times as possible, until the mind fully accepts its truth and you find yourself speaking and acting in its consciousness.)

I am a Son of God, a Spiritual Being, living always in the Kingdom of Divine Mind. In this, My true consciousness, there is for Me no lack or limitation of any good thing.

From My human mind's viewpoint, however, there is no direct evidence of this. Yet I am teaching it through long, hard experience, bringing to it much struggle, suffering and failure, that the human self of itself is nothing, can have nothing, can do nothing, and that I am all that it is; that I give it all that it ever gets, and empower it to do all that it ever does.

So that now it is learning that it is not, and that I alone am; that I as a Son of God know all things and have all power; that whatever the Father has, the Son has; and likewise what the Son has, his human reflection must have; that it therefore has it always, has all good things ever available—when it comes back into My consciousness and sees there with My eyes.

From this it glimpses that it is but an instrument that I am preparing, purifying and perfecting through these experiences, apparently getting it ready for some use I intend to make of it later.

It is thus realizing that with My being a Son of God and thereby having all things, I naturally have no desire and no need, except that of expressing My perfect life through it—My human self, and if it feels a desire or a need, it is but an indication that the thing desired is about to manifest. Otherwise it would not be felt.

That being so, it is gradually realizing that for it also there is no need, all good things being always present, and it is learning to let go of its personal ideas, desires and opinions, and to go about its business unconcerned, knowing that all needed things will be taken care of and provided by Me, as surely as the lungs will receive air in the next breath.

It is likewise learning to pay no attention to appearances, that what seems real and important to the outer senses are but thought-pictures formed in the mind and which, if good, fall far short of the goodness and perfection that are ever seen in Divine Mind; or if bad or undesirable, such do not exist—except in the mortal mind.

Therefore it is perceiving that in order to see the Truth it has but to close its mortal eyes and mind and to look with the eyes of Spirit—My eyes, when all the riches and glories of the Kingdom shine forth and are clearly visible.

When one thus sees Reality all the illusions of Separation disappear, even as when looking at the sun there are no shadows—all is light.

II. KINGDOM

PAPER No. 35 NOVEMBER, 1931

Many who receive this Paper are becoming aware of their Brothers in Christ, both those dwelling in the flesh and those in Spirit. Not necessarily do they actually see them or hear them speak, for that is not essential to one in the Christ Consciousness. There is a Spiritual knowing that is far superior to what is reported by the senses—even by the soul senses.

Likewise there are many who have either recently entered the Kingdom, or are able to look in, as it were, and who are more or less aware of the wonders existing there and long for a clearer sight and understanding of what they there see. For as we previously stated, because everything there is almost the opposite of all things seen and known in the mortal consciousness, they are but as babes in understanding in the new consciousness.

This cannot help but be when it is realized that all that is seen in the outer world are creations of the mortal mind, that which thinks itself a self and separate from God's Mind; and hence all its creations are built of the darkness of its sense of separation, of living outside of God's Love and Wisdom and therefore of not expecting any help from Him. Hence all are built for self, to gratify and benefit self, and are largely selfish. All of man's creations, all of his institutions, commercial, industrial, financial, social, educational and even philanthropical and spiritual, are built upon and to feed and perpetuate selfishness. Investigate carefully and impersonally and you cannot but see that this is true, especially when compared with what exists in the Kingdom of Divine Mind.

What do we see there? That which strikes us first is the exquisite beauty of everything and everyone, that all are perfect even as the Father conceived them, every soul young, happy and radiant, and everything devised for the free use and enjoyment of the inhabitants. Which means that there is a rich abundance of all good things for everyone always available. No one there ever needs anything, for it is always at hand. A desire for anything -is immediately fulfilled. Then of course no one needs to ask or take from another, and no one ever owes another anything. Hence money is not known there. Everyone has everything he wants, because all he has to do is to see clearly in his mind what he wants, and it takes shape and substance right before his eyes, ready and perfect for his use.

From this you can see there is no selfishness there, for all there are those in whom self no longer is. There is no injustice, for the law of justice rules everyone's consciousness. There is no evil, for it has been learned that evil, sin, sickness, inharmony and unhappiness are only the creations of mortal mind, and of course one who is selfless never thinks and thereby creates such things.

Does this help you to see how and why man is responsible for the outer world that it is his own creation —not God's creation? And can you now see what is God's world His Kingdom, your heavenly home, where you can return anytime you will by knowing and seeing only the truth and thinking true thoughts—His thoughts —about yourself and about Him and His world?

For His world—your real home—is here, all about you, now, and is clearly visible to those who have eyes to see. But you cannot see it or your brothers there with your mortal eyes. You must look with your inner eyes, which enable you to see right through outer appearances the soul of people and things.

The beautiful part of it all is that they are there whether you see them or not these others who have found God within themselves, have found there a new and wonderful self, a wonderful world, and wonderful comrades in it, a world far more real than the everchanging one without.

Yes, they have found their eternal home, the Kingdom of God's Consciousness, the same home which Jesus described in His many parables, when trying to tell of it to the people of His day; and where He went after His earthly mission was accomplished, and where He now lives and works among His disciples who have followed Him there. To them He is a very real and actual Teacher, Guide and Friend, who is preparing them for the great day when He will make Himself manifest to all His followers on earth and will bring Heaven down to earth to be truly in the midst of men.

It is under His direction that we are preparing you, dear friends, for that day; preparing you so that you can not only follow Him there, but that you can be aware of Him and of the soul world now, every moment of the day; can consciously live there even while your body is still in the physical world. For where your consciousness is, there you are. And you can center your consciousness in your self-created body of flesh, or in your Spiritual body, the one formed in the image and likeness of God, whichever you will—when you know the truth of your divine nature.

Our part is to teach you that truth, as you have found during the months- you have been traveling with us. And we have now brought you face to face with the fact that you, in your real nature, are a Son of God, a Spiritual being, and that as such you must bring your human mind to a full realization of that fact, in order that you may lift its consciousness into oneness with your soul consciousness.

Now let us show you what that means. You are a Son of God, descended from your divine estate into your human soul in order to redeem it and bring its consciousness back into your divine consciousness. You have brought it up to the stage of discipleship, where it is aware of you dwelling within itself and now actually living your life in it and directing all of its activities both in the soul world and in the outer world of the human mind.

Your main work now is the cleansing of that mind of all its untrue thoughts and beliefs gained from wrong teaching of parents, school, church, books and teachers, about life, your own nature, and God. All of these teachings have been mainly wrong and almost the exact opposite of the truth found in the real world of the soul, the Kingdom consciousness of God's Mind, where you as a soul live, move and have your being, as we have shown above. And finally, those of you who have traveled all the way with us have eliminated from your minds most of the wrong beliefs about self and most of self's creations, so that your minds are now ready to let go and yield themselves over to you and permit you to use them as the selfless instruments you have been preparing and fitting them to be from the beginning.

You are therefore almost ready to bring the consciousness of your human mind back into oneness with your soul consciousness. So that the two will be one and you can then be aware of all that is manifesting on the soul plane of expression. But before that can be we must need further prepare you by making you definitely aware of yourself as a soul apart and distinct from the consciousness of your human mind.

You in your integrity as a soul are pure conscious ness. In other words, you are that which is conscious or aware of all that comes to you from without through the avenue of your five senses, or through vibrations which they are not sensitive enough to perceive, such as impressions or thoughts from other centers of consciousness. All of these sensations and vibrations are interpreted to your consciousness through the of your human mind.

But as a soul or consciousness you are distinct from your human mind, for it serves merely as an instrument to receive and inform you of what comes from without in the world of matter. Yet your mind is in reality an outer extension of your soul consciousness, slowed down to the mental capacity of your human brain, there serving as your agent in the informing you of all things going on in the physical world. and of carrying out your instructions pertaining to that world.

In that partial and necessarily limited consciousness your mind grew to think itself -a self and separate from you in your soul consciousness. In this fancied separateness it gradually filled its consciousness with all those wrong concepts and beliefs about physical and mental things spoken of above, and which grew so real and tangible in its consciousness that in time they ruled all your thoughts, speech and actions.

But these concepts and beliefs should have no influence over your soul consciousness—only as you let them. The proof is, when you get quiet and still your mind and shut out all thoughts and impressions coming from without, then you are in your pure soul consciousness and are free to be aware of the impressions coming from within your soul. For then you learn that deep within the soul there is -a higher consciousness and a Spiritual intelligence that press against the soul from within informing you of Spiritual things, even as the outer mind's consciousness presses from without to inform you of material things. That higher or innermost consciousness is that of your Higher or Divine Self, a Son of God.

This enables you to see how you, as a Son of God, reach down or out from the center of your being in Divine Consciousness into the soul consciousness, and thence outward into the mortal mind, giving to your brain its consciousness, which causes it to think itself separate, when it is only the consciousness of God thinned down to the brain mind's capacity to hold and use it.

It likewise enables you to see that as a soul and with your human mind realizing your true nature and the true world you live in, your mind is then prepared and should be ready to become aware of the soul world and all in it. In other words, with your mind cleansed of all its old mental creations—all its beliefs and thought pictures of things in the seemingly outer world and which before it thought so real and important, it should gradually become conscious of the soul or inner and true nature of these things and of the people around you.

As we have said before, all true disciples are due to come into this awareness any time, and as a help we urge that from now on you meditate much on the idea of being a soul, trying to throw off all that presses upon your consciousness from the outer world of mind and to retire into and remain back in your soul consciousness, watching and noting all that comes to you there, in order that you may learn all about this new world. You will find by being alert you ᶳwill receive ample instruction and direction regarding what appears.

But try to realize that what you see will not be as you saw before. You now use a new and entirely different set of faculties, for you are dealing with realities that exist in a new consciousness, manifesting in a different and much higher rate of vibration. In this new consciousness, perception will be of a different kind. In fact, some of you will see them purely as ideas or as a knowing what they are, instead of "seeing" anything. This knowing will be far more accurate and real than any seeing of forms or hearing of voices could be, if you can realize it; for in pure knowing is included all that your five senses could tell you and a thousand times more.

Some of you, however, if you are psychic, will have these truths illustrated to you in visions or mental pictures. But always seek to know their inner meaning, for pictures are of no value unless you understand their meaning and purpose. This will be given to your mind, if it refuses to be satisfied with mere pictures. Naturally it is the knowing faculty, which is purely Spiritual, that should be sought. The other is but an interesting side issue, and may prove to be a snare to entangle you in the joys of the "Summerland" and prevent your reaching the true goal. By persisting, the consciousness will continue to unfold however, until it reaches union with its Source your Divine Consciousness, where all is known and where everything needed will flow naturally and instantly to you.

Above all things try to realize that you are a , Son of God, a Spiritual being, living as a soul in an ideal body in a realm of consciousness called the Kingdom Of God which is the real world of being. If you only know it, it is just as easy and will make you far happier than believing you are a human being living as a self in an imperfect physical body in a realm of consciousness called the material world, which is an unreal world that has no existence except as a belief of the mortal mind.

We ask you not only to realize yourself as actually living in this ideal soul body and soul world, but that they are very real and are where you would be in consciousness were you to be released from your physical body, or were to "die." As your human mind becomes more and more freed from its illusions and misconceptions and thus becomes able to perceive the truth of the real world of this Kingdom, your inner eyes will open and you will be seeing and be conscious of living in two worlds at the same time.

And do you not now see that when you can rise entirely out of the consciousness of your human mind into that of your soul and can remain there at will—you are actually in the soul world, just as much as if you had died to the physical world? For are you not where your consciousness is?

And can you not see what this means that by rising into the soul consciousness, you then will be able to learn how to rule all in the physical world, moulding its conditions by thought like unto the conditions you see in the real world and which you now wish to obtain in the outer world of the mind?

But of this we will speak further in the next article when dealing with the subject of consciousness. At present meditate much upon what is stated above, trying daily to enter and abide in your soul consciousness, so that you can become wholly familiar with the reality of the soul world and know it for what it is your true home, your Father's House, where we have been leading you all these months and which you have finally reached.

CONSCIOUSNESS

We showed you that by rising into your soul consciousness and becoming accustomed -to it, you can learn how to rule things and conditions in the physical world —by means of thought.

In the soul world everything is formed by thought even as in the physical. But while in the physical world thought directs the use of the physical material that has first to be secured and out of which the desired thing is built, in the soul world (in both the astral and the mental realms) the material is naturally of an astral or mental nature, which is altogether under the control of thought and can be formed and shaped by merely thinking it into any desired form and condition.

In order to give you an idea of our meaning, but not asking you to accept what is stated other than it is claimed to come from a little girl spirit attending on the Spirit -side of life the seances of a noted medium,, we quote from a book entitled "The Spirit World," by Mrs. M. T. Longley:

"We will now relate some of the teachings and statements of Nannie, told in her artless simplicity, which gained credence for them in the minds of all who listened to her tales.

"Relating the instances of her wonderful school life (in the soul realm), she told of the manner of work and teachings therein. Lessons are both subjective "and objective. The pupil must first be taught to perceive the thought clearly in the mind, picture it mentally to himself, and then produce it in the outer atmosphere. Said the little prattler:

We can make a lily or a rose, but we must first think of it so we can mentally see the flower; then we must learn to concentrate the mind on that and nothing else. We must learn about vibration and how to harmonize with the vibration of the rose or the lily, then how to gather the forces of the flower from the atmosphere.

'The teacher shows us how by her own work. She gathers a lot of mist out of the atmosphere and works it with her hands till it gets thicker and more like sub, stance. At first it is thin and finer than steam, but she works it till it grows more substantial and just as she wants it to fashion into form, all the time breathing on it and thinking of the color she wants—pink or red or some other color. She keeps her mind all the time on the appearance, texture and hue of the flower she wants it to be while moulding it into shape. Her breathing on it helps to make the color and the perfume of the flower, and she does the work in a minute or two very quickly. No one can tell it from. a real flower.

"We children have to learn all this, but we like it; it's real play, and sometimes it's funny too; for we don't always remember to think rose or lily, or whatever it is we want, and the thing becomes broken or out of shape and fades right away, and then the teacher says we haven't concentrated properly.'

"When older, she told of other methods of concentration and work. The teacher said the children must learn to produce something like a picture or an article without drawing perceptibly from the vital forces outside themselves. For instance, to simplify matters, the teacher caused a sheet of porcelain-like substance to appear before the class, something for them to concentrate their minds toward; then they were each in turn to think some object on the sheet. One selected to produce a red rose, one a bird, one a star, and so on. Nannie said for some time she had trouble. She tried a star and it was 'wobbly;' a flower and it was broken; a bird and it was upside down, although the colors of each were good. The teacher said Nannie let her mind wander, did not fix it closely enough on her subject.

"Nannie told that as the atmosphere contains the ethereal essence of all substances, it is not difficult to gather them for use, and they often gathered color and sweets from flowers and the atmosphere to form sugar balls and other shapes for the delectation of the children. She said they sometimes teased 'Tela, or someone else, to make us a nice ice cream or pudding or cake all white and shining;' and the culinary artist would proceed to do so—not with pots and pans, and flour and eggs, and things of that sort; but simply by knowing how to manipulate the atmosphere, draw from it the essentials needed and bring them to the right consistency and degree of perfection, the cake, cream, pudding, or candy would be made and enjoyed to the satisfaction of the guests or children.

"She said, and other spirits told us the same, that persons coming into the Spirit world with the sensations of hunger or starvation are cured of their hunger by attendants or caretakers, who know how, drawing essentials from the atmosphere, manipulating and adding personal magnetism to them and producing an appetizing piece of meat all cooked ready for eating that never vibrated in the body of any animal, but which looks as if it did, tastes the same, and does better work for the partaker who cannot tell that he is not eating a bit from the choice part of a well-fed animal."

Remember that the above tells what is taught children who live in the soul realm. Later through the power of concentration and clear visualizing they learn to create objects at will without manipulating with their hands; one watching would see them take form right before their eyes out of the atmosphere. As the ethereal essence of all substance is contained in the atmosphere, one who knows that, through the power of his will and his directing thought can draw forth whatever he needs.

Try to realize that if children on the higher planes of Spirit are taught these laws, old souls should know them and are probably employing them in their work on those planes. Which means that you, who are disciples of Christ, and who are old souls and live on the highest of the soul planes, should know perfectly how to use these laws and are now trying to teach the right use of them to your brain minds.

That you do know how to use them is plain from the fact of your human reflections having misused this knowledge in the past in the creation of conditions which are now reacting upon them because of the selfishness which motivated them in such creation. The time is now here when you are calling upon your human selves to rectify these mistakes, by willingly returning to your soul - consciousness and from there creating the outer conditions which they now know alone will bring peace and happiness into their lives and into a world sorely distressed on account of the mistakes of the past.

You have been shown how to do this in Paper No. 25, in the Way Out article. We are now explaining why, when you do as instructed, results must follow. For the soul realm is the real world and the real creating is done there. Anything or any condition created there by thought and held in consciousness as being finished MUST outmanifest itself.

Then it behooves every disciple of Christ, to begin now to create carefully in his human mind, filling in every detail, the true and permanent conditions he sees in his higher consciousness and which he wants to outmanifest. And when all is clearly visible and you know it is FIN' ISHED, go about your business in the serene assurance that the condition thus created now exists; mentally see it as actually being so and yourself happily a part of it in the outer world, naturally allowing not the slightest doubt of it to enter your consciousness, and it will soon outmanifest and establish itself in your life.

If you do all that we have here stated, the results must follow; for it is the law, and the law never fails.

BRINGING THE KINGDOM DOWN TO EARTH

In view of what has been stated, it should be Seen that now that the way has been shown, it becomes the duty of every conscious disciple of

Christ receiving this Paper to apply the above instruction to the rectifying of present wrong conditions in the world of men's consciousness.

This instruction has been given you to USE—not only to adjust your own affairs to the true state of being you see existing in your higher consciousness, but to help your Brothers in Spirit bring the full light of Divine Mind down into the consciousness of as many human minds as can be quickened to receive it.

With our help your human mind has been quickened. It now knows that the real world is not what the physical senses report, but is the perfect world of the soul realm. Therefore it must cease recognizing the outer world as real, must cease believing you have any part in it or in the conditions manifesting there, must refuse to let such conditions enter its consciousness, knowing that you are a Son of God, a Spiritual Being, dwelling in a perfect world where such things do not exist.

This must be evident to everyone who reads, and hence you are now ready for definite work. Go back and read carefully the above, and then what follows, until you gather the full significance of it all, and you will see wherein your real duty lies.

The time has come for you to begin actual service as a member of the Brotherhood, for as a disciple you are actually a member. You have entered Its consciousness; therefore Its help is always available. Christ love has now become your life; hence His wisdom and power are ever yours when needed in His service. His service is the helping and blessing of others.

Knowing this, then your first duty is to keep your consciousness clean of all untrue thoughts, and to carry in it only those that pertain to your Real Self and your Real World. In other words, you must learn to live in your soul consciousness which is now the Christ 'Consciousness, shutting out all that would push through from the outer mind.

And your next duty is to refrain from voicing anything about outer conditions that is not good and perfect, no matter what others say to the contrary. You simply know the truth, and let others believe and say what they will. For while your ears may hear, your mind need not listen. You must train your mind to observe strictly this rule.

By thus always knowing the truth—the truth that only God's perfect world exists, peopled only by His children who love Him and are doing all that they do to please Him you are carrying about a great light that will illumine the world consciousness far and wide, quickening and lighting many other minds and thus gradually driving out all darkness in the consciousness of your com ᵖ munity. For can you not see that the greater this knowing, the more powerful becomes your light and the more far-reaching its radiance?

Imagine every soul receiving these teachings becoming such a light, going about letting it shine into the hearts and lives of all they contact,— think of the mighty influence they will radiate!

But remember, they are doing nothing, only serving as outposts, or channels, through which the Brotherhood of Christ is pouring the Great Light of Christ Love down into the consciousness of men, driving out the darkness of ignorance from which was born their sense of self and separation.

This is our part, dear ones, and there is no greater work that we can do—link ourselves through our minds with the consciousness of our Brothers in Spirit who are serving under our blessed Leader and Saviour Christ Jesus.

And this we must do now that we may quickly become perfect in our knowing; for we are soon to engage in a mighty struggle with the powers of darkness that are seeking to gain control of the whole world of men's minds,

accounting for the increased darkness manifesting at present in world conditions. In fact the battle has already begun and before it is over they will seemingly have gained almost complete control.

But all we have to do is to know who we are and of what we are a part—that WE ARE THE LIGHT, and can the darkness prevail against the light?

Therefore be not anxious about the future, for- the future must be of the light when the darkness is all dispelled; and that will surely be, for it is so ordained by our loving Father-God. In the meantime all that need concern you is that you are always walking and serving in the Light of His Love, and all else will be taken care of. FOR HE WILL TAKE CARE -OF HIS OWN.

III. THE LIGHT

PAPER No. 36, Dec. 1931.

In this Paper, the third anniversary of the inauguration of this particular phase of the Master's Work, and likewise in the month that is- the anniversary of His birth, we can find no more fitting way to celebrate than to talk about the wonderful Light He brought to . the world of men's minds.

Remember, while He brought . to us the Light, -He brought it because He is the Light. St. John truly tells us this in the first chapter of his Gospel; how in Him was the Light of men and that Light is ever shining in the darkness; but the darkness of men's intellects prevent them from comprehending Him and thereby from-knowing- that -He alone can lead them out of the darkness into the light they seek. And they do not comprehend because man's intellect cannot understand how Jesus can be the Word, the Logos, the Light of men and also be the man of Galilee, the Son of Joseph and Mary, a man like unto us. For John quite plainly intimated that He was both man and God.

Let us look closely at John's words. In the first sentence he says:

"In the beginning was the Word, and the Word was with God, and the Word was God."

In view of what he later states, this can mean nothing less than that Jesus is not only the Word or Logos, but is God, Himself. And as we know that God -is the source of all life, and John says that life is the -light of men, it can only mean that Jesus in some mystical -way must be God, come forth into the world to manifest Himself as The Light. That makes it not difficult to realize that Light as being the wondrous truth that Jesus radiated in His life and actions and gave forth in His living words, and which has so penetrated the darkness of men's consciousness during the past 1900 years that His Light has now reached to the uttermost parts of the earth.

Yes, despite the seeming great darkness that is now manifesting in the-whole world, the Light of Christ is so powerful and potent that before very long it will utterly dispel the darkness, proving the truth of the saying that it is darkest just before dawn.'

Can you grasp that? It must be only because of the presence of a powerful light that it is now so dark. A powerful light always makes the darkest shadows. But when that light is brought close, it diffuses itself so that it overspreads everything and drives out all darkness.

Just that is taking place now. The light has become so powerful, because the Innumerable Host of the Forces of Light is approaching close to the earth from the Inner Realms, and is so illumining the minds of the children of light, that the brilliance of Their radiance is rapidly dispelling any darkness still existing in the minds of Christ's disciples, and causing all outer darkness to concentrate now only in massed shadows ready for the final conflict between light and darkness, and which makes that darkness appear darker than it really is. And who will say there can be any other outcome than victory for the Forces of Light?

Make no mistake, those Forces are close, very close. Many have seen Them; many are actually seeing the gathering of the great army of the Lord, clad all in white, in white armour, on white horses, with white banners flying and with faces lit with divine ardor, knowing what the result of the coming battle will mean to the world—the freeing it from sin, sickness and death forever, permitting the Kingdom to manifest on earth even as it is in heaven.

We tell you this now so that you may consciously prepare for your part in what awaits. In the November Paper we said YOU ARE THE LIGHT—you who are conscious disciples off-Christ."

From what you have learned in the last few Papers, you are now ready to take up real work, for you are able to bring your mind's consciousness back into your true consciousness—back into its light, where it sees and knows the truth, knows that all that is without is darkness, because born of the mind's belief in separation from God's Consciousness.

Knowing now that you are the light, part of that same light which Jesus was and is—for is He not back within and a part of that same Consciousness where You are—then the God of you can shine through, can take charge, and do all the work you came here to do. Remember, your mind has given to Him its perfect trust. Therefore, all you need do is to let Him have complete charge, to trust Him fully, and thus let your light shine.

Yes, that is all you need do—to have your mind know the truth and hold itself ever in its light, to trust perfectly, and let the Christ of you do what He will with and through you. Then can you not see that it is through you and all disciples of Christ that the Forces of Light will accomplish what they are come down to earth to do? For remember your Higher Self is a soldier of this Army of Light, is one of these Sons of God! They can work only through Their human expressions.

Now you can see why we have been to all these pains to lead your minds out of the darkness of self's wrong beliefs- into the light of your Christ Consciousness. We have come "to bear witness of the Light, that all men through Him might believe.

Like John, the Messenger, in our outer selves we are not that Light, but we were "sent to bear witness of that Light—the true Light which lighteth every man that cometh into the world.

"He came to His own, and few of His own received Him. But as many as did receive Him, to them gave He power to become Sons of God, even to them that believe on His Name.

Remember, we are speaking of that Light which Jesus was and which we are in our True Selves, that Light which shines in the darkness of our human personalities —the Light of our Christ Self, the Holy Spirit of God which lighteth every man that cometh into the world.

For even as Jesus was God's Spirit, the Christ, in expression, so are we; for. is not God All in All? The only difference is that Jesus knew His Godhood, His Oneness with the Father, and through that knowing He gave to the world the Light it was then ready to receive. And ever since His Light, through the Truth which He taught and manifested, has been the Light that has lighted men's minds down through the centuries— those that received and followed Him. And to all who received Him, that is, received the truth of the Christ Spirit being both God in Jesus and God in them, He—the Holy Spirit in them gave the power to know they were Sons of God; even to those who believe in His Name, or who enter their Christ Consciousness and know their Oneness with Him.

From this you will have perceived that by the Light is meant the Christ Consciousness or the Holy Spirit of God, which dwells deep within the soul consciousness of every man, even though man does not know it. But you know it, and now we will -show you another way you can contact and receive from that Consciousness.

Many of you have had the experience when meditating in the Silence of finding before you could perfectly still your mind, there would flow into it things you had for gotten or neglected to do, or you would be given a clear glimpse of the solution of some problem facing you, or the whereabouts of something -lost. In other words, your mind now being quiet, it seemed to draw to itself the things you needed to know.

Where did these things come from? Whence come the ideas to the inventor, the ideal pictures to the mind of the artist, the inspiration to the poet, and the ability to express harmony to the musician? Many of these are inspired by mentors on the inner planes of being, you will say. And truly, for every soul has mentors and teachers in the unseen who are ever helping them, when it is possible to get inspiration through to their minds. But back of them are the Higher Selves of every soul, Who in turn inspire and direct these helpers to do all that they do for Their respective souls. But when a soul has evolved spiritually to the stage. where the Higher Self descends and takes up His abode within- the soul and no longer overshadows it "from above," then the Higher Self becomes the sole inner Teacher and Authority, and the soul knows this and causes its human mind to become more or less conscious of His Presence and to turn more and more within to Him for guidance and instruction.

This as you know is the stage of discipleship, and after much experience in meditation -and receiving such guidance, gradually the disciple finds himself drawn within into the Consciousness of the Higher Self where he is given to see with His eyes and to know with His understanding such things as he needs to know.

You have been told this before and many of you are able to enter that Consciousness, but now we wish you to realize clearly what takes place when you enter your Higher Self's or the Christ Consciousness.

We have called it the Christ Consciousness, and that must mean that in that Consciousness you then know your Oneness with the Father. In other words, you have entered the Kingdom of Divine Mind and are in the Father's Consciousness, where you can tune in, as it were, with anything you need to know for does not the Father know all- things?

But how can you tune in and thus receive anything you need to know? In just the way we described above and which is employed by every inventor, artist, poet, musician, and every disciple of Christ, whether -or not they know the process we shall now describe.

You will remember the experience, while meditating, of forgotten things and those you needed to do flowing into your mind as it grew quiet, and reminding you of them. Just as your mind by being stilled thus releases your consciousness from outer things are the unfinished and needed things of your consciousness likewise released. For in the soul or pure consciousness, as we have shown, everything is perfect and in purest harmony. There? fore, when no longer interfered with by the outer mind, whatever is needed to restore harmony is released and flows into your consciousness.

Likewise if there is anything you need to know and which will restore harmony when known, then all that you need do is to focus -your deep interest and attention upon that thing and to hold your consciousness alert, as if it were a funnel into which will be poured the knowledge you seek, knowing that by so doing, when impelled by strong desire, you tune in. with its vibration and it thus becomes one with your consciousness and will flow instantly to you." With practice, by such concentrated knowing and desiring, you become a powerful attracting magnet which will draw to you all things you need to know and have.

The reason that' this results is that all is consciousness —that there is nothing that is not an idea in conscious ness, and every idea is naturally a center of consciousness. Ideas differ only in their rates of vibration. Therefore when you tune in to and become harmonized with the vibration of any given idea, you instantly become one with its consciousness and everything -you need to know about it will flow from it into your mind.

When you have learned by practice 'to do this, and it is possible to do it in this particular way only by a disciple, you will find it will come to you as a memory of something recalled from the storehouse of mind; it will come as a flash of illumination, as if a light poured into your mind and you to "see" or remember and again know.

This is entirely different from so-called inspiration, which implies that some other mind inspires or pours thoughts or words into your mind. And it is far- different from automatic writing, or definite teachings- in actual' words given you by invisible helpers. These come from mentors or teachers who are with you to help you just to the extent you make it possible, and you receive this help only when they can give it to you.

The other way you get it through your own efforts direct from the one source—Divine Mind—of which you know your consciousness is a part - and with- which it is- always connected. So you can always receive from It whatever you need and at any time.

You will note that above we said that this knowledge came from the - storehouse of mind—that you remembered and KNEW, How could you know if you had not learned it before? -Why of course you know, for are you not a Son of God, Who with all your Brothers provide the consciousness. of all men of earth—for are They not responsible for the earth and its humanity—and in Whose consciousness dwells all knowledge pertaining -to earth and even of those realms beyond the earth up to and including the Sun, the abode- of :God, Their. Father?

In other words, as a Son" of God, God's Consciousness is your consciousness as it is your Brothers' consciousness, and all in that Consciousness is always available to you when you are able to connect up with it, as we have shown. Therefore you are One of Those Who Know, not one of those who have to be taught or told. Of course, however, you, yourself, must know this. But we have told you, and 'if something within responds, it is time for you to realize its truth and for you to assume your real nature and to begin to think, speak and act as a conscious Son of God.

This brings us back to the Light. For in the consciousness of your real nature, that of a Son of God, you are living in the Light. In that consciousness all is Light, for that consciousness is the Light. It .is the Source, the Essence, the Real of all Light. It is God's Conscious- ness, the Sun of all being. In that Consciousness then there is no slightest shadow, for its Light is so powerful and perfect -that all God knows is plainly seen, known and is naturally the consciousness of all who are in its Light.

From this you can understand what is the true Light, that Light whose ray is shining in the darkness of every man. For as all is Consciousness and there is only one Consciousness and that Consciousness is the innermost of all human minds, which are but the outermost expressions of that Consciousness, you can now see how that Light is ever shining deep back within every soul, even if the mind never comprehends it.

But what is the occasion for that Consciousness-expressing Itself on this dark planet earth in the minds of men? It is because of God's Love for His Sons and for His Son's sons, that they may receive of His Life and may have it abundantly. Therefore He has been pouring Che Light of His Love from the beginning through the hearts of His Sons, giving Them the fullness of His Life and power, so that They in Their turn can so quicken the consciousness of Their sons that the spark of light in their souls will glow and increase until it permits Them to enter and abide in its light and make of them living and immortal souls. Gradually, one by -one, are They thus quickening and entering the souls of men, and Their Light is spreading over the earth, until it will no longer be known among its sister orbs in the firmament of the heavens as the little red planet, but its light will shine with equal brilliancy with theirs and it will take its place along side of them in the Holy Fraternity of the Celestial Spheres.

And who are these Sons of. God, also called Sons of Light and Sons of Mind .by those who know? We have told you how in the beginning They came here to re deem the earth, Their own progeny; how under the leadership of Their Great Elder Brother, called The Christ, otherwise The Light, They descended from the Light of the Sun of God's Mind, bringing Their Light to-quicken the light in the consciousness of every man upon the earth, to stay with these men, Their own children, until their consciousness had been lifted up into the light of . Their Consciousness and finally into the Light of Their Father- God's Consciousness.

Can you see now how Jesus the Christ, Himself, finally came to earth in His Own Person to shed sufficient of His Light into the minds of men that It will remain and be the quickening power ever coming from without— as the truth He taught and the example of His Life He brought—to fan the spark of spirit within into a flame and thereby cause the souls of men to awaken and listen, to understand and know the voice of the Christ, their Higher Self, when He -speaks from within their hearts? Christ then is God's Holy Spirit, His Divine Love, the Light made manifest upon earth, and now- coming into evidence in -the hearts and lives of the many men who listen to and follow His leading. He is not -only The Light that has shone down through the centuries as Jesus the Christ, and is now shining in all His pristine glory in the soul and higher realms of the Kingdom, but He is The Light that is shining in the heart of every man that has opened his heart to Love. For He is the Light of Love, and every man who knows and follows Love, knows our blessed Master Jesus and follows Him and is known and loved by Him.

THE LAW OF HARMONY

In Paper 33, we promised to give definite instructions how to speak effectively to the cells of your body, to your human mind, and to your soul, so that they will always render perfect service and produce for you any desired results.

In that article, we showed you how all consciousness in your body, mind and soul is your consciousness, but it is also God's; and in the article above we showed you how to tune in to the consciousness of any other idea or center of consciousness. Likewise how in your soul or pure consciousness everything is perfect and in purest harmony, and that when you can free your consciousness from all awareness of outer things and can enter that soul consciousness of harmony, all the things causing inharmony would be released in the outer world of mind, and whatever, is needed to restore harmony would flow naturally and immediately to you. This is so because it is the law of harmony.

Try to realize that the universe of God's world, -with its many celestial and solar systems, operates under this same law of harmony; that should any one factor in the universe be out of harmony, it would disrupt the whole system and produce chaos. This means that you in reality are not out of harmony with it; that you must be doing what you do in accordance with the operation of this immutable law of harmony.

Then what is it that appears so glaringly to you to be inharmony— what about pain, disease, poverty, crime, and unhappiness? Have we not told you that these exist only because of -the wrong understanding and the untrue thoughts and feelings man persists in indulging in and in carrying around in his consciousness? They only appear to be out of harmony because of man's ignorance -of the law, and his not knowing that what appears is but the law of harmony operating in the keeping of every part of the universe always in perfect balance. If one swerves in his thinking from -the perfect harmony of Divine Mind, action immediately and automatically sets up in the human - consciousness and -causes what seems to be a disturbance of the existing harmony; when in fact - it is but a-switching or counterbalancing of forces in order to preserve and maintain that harmony. In other words the law of harmony is always exerting pressure to force the consciousness back into its perfect state, and what seems to be inharmony is only the feeling caused by harmony pressing itself back into expression. Study this carefully until you get all of. its inner meaning and application.

When you get it, you will see that when man again thinks true thoughts the supposedly inharmonious elements or conditions will instantly -and automatically right themselves.

Now let us see how we can apply this law to the freeing of your consciousness of wrong outer things, especially when there is pain, disease, or suffering of any kind.

First you must realize there is only one way, and that is by deliberately and determinedly picturing and seeing in your mind the opposite and the perfection of what' ever is causing the pain, disease or suffering. If there is pain or disease in the body, picture perfect health, strength and harmony there. If there is mental suffering caused by conditions in your home or affairs, picture the opposite of such conditions and see them manifesting perfectly and ideally, and yourself enjoying them to the

Yes, you must actually do this—there is no other way to free yourself to rise out of the untrue consciousness in which you had allowed your interest to become involved.

Remember, you are a soul or pure consciousness, and are not your physical body in its imperfect state as your human mind now sees it, and which has no part in your soul consciousness.

But you, who have accompanied us all these months, have long since gained such control of your mind that you can even in pain turn your attention away from it to anything you will. By thus filling your mind with these perfect pictures, you find that two things are accomplished you counteract the effects of the wrong suggestions instilled into the cell consciousness of that part of your body where is the pain, flooding its consciousness with the light of truth; and you actually retire back into your soul consciousness where only harmony, purity and perfection exist; thereby bringing the consciousness of both the cells- of your body and of your mind into the harmony of your soul consciousness.

When through practice you are able to prove this, you will see for yourself how the law of harmony operates; how, when you have brought your mind and its consciousness, which controls the consciousness of the cells of your body, into perfect harmony with your soul consciousness —which remember, you being a disciple, is now one with your Christ Consciousness—all seemingly inharmonious elements and conditions in the outer are released, and there flows into their place harmonious and happy elements, thus restoring all to their proper and natural condition.

No, it will not be easy to prove this—it takes practice and failure to entitle you to enjoy its fruits, which are freedom and self-mastery, and which mean mastery over body, mind and soul. And you must do all that we have indicated; such fruits. are not for the weak-minded or the easily discouraged, but only for determined and unconquerable souls.

In order to help, we are glad to give you some further suggestions. For instance, speak from the consciousness inspired by. the truth we have declared to the cells of any part of your body in which there is pain or inharmony, as follows:

'Listen, my children! You are centers of my consciousness—not of that of my mortal mind, but of my soul consciousness. My soul is the outer reflection of God's Consciousness, even as you are the outer reflection of my consciousness. This makes your consciousness a part of mine, and mine a part of God's, and means that your consciousness is actually God's consciousness.

"Now -think! We see and know you as Perfect—just as He created you in the beginning—in His image and likeness. So know that you are not as my mind has wrongly believed and held you to be in the past—weak, sick or in pain,' but you are strong and healthy and are functioning always in perfect harmony.

"Know the truth, my children, and be FREE! Free from all sense of separateness and error forever."

Speaking these words of truth with positiveness and in the knowing of their truth will surely bring harmony to the cell consciousness that before recognized and reported pain; because through the power of pure truth its consciousness has been lifted up to your consciousness which dwells in the light of truth. And just as long as the cell consciousness is not dragged down again by your mind's memory of that pain or even the thought of it, there will be harmony in that part of the body.

MIND KNOWING AND SOUL KNOWING

This brings us to the consideration of a very important factor in the "knowing of truth.' Have you grasped as yet the real purpose why we have tried so hard to explain and to reason out all these inner truths step by step to you, so that you are now accepting them as spiritual FACTS?

It is in order that your mind, which means its consciousness, will accept them. When it actually accepts and fully understands, they become a part of its consciousness, and sink into its sub-consciousness, where they automatically come forth for use whenever needed.

You will remember, as a Son of God, you already know these truths in your soul consciousness, but through these Papers you have been unfolding them to your mortal mind—and for no other purpose than for their use by your human personality, or that you can use them through it; for not until there has been brought about a union of its understanding with yours of course it would hinder and limit their use. Therefore, what you as a Son of God have been doing from the beginning has been to bring the consciousness of your human mind into oneness with your consciousness, by teaching it through life's lessons the truth of its being —that it is not separate or different, weak, poor, sick, limited or lacking in any way, but that there is only one consciousness, one self, one life—yours, which is one with your Father-God's in Heaven. We have been helping by teaching and impressing these truths upon your mind ever since you came with us.

Now let us see if we can tell you why the necessity of so teaching your human mind, when you know its truth in your soul. Can you not now see that all that is without exists only in the mortal mind's consciousness as picture-beliefs in their reality, and as they thus appear are not at all in your soul consciousness. where everything is ideal, all good and all perfect? Then is it not absolutely necessary to cleanse your mind of all these untrue beliefs and replace them with the truths we have been so insistently pointing out to you, before it can come into your consciousness and see and know as you know?

All its life your human reflection has believed in and has been fed upon error, until it has become completely involved in a false consciousness which it has thought to be real. All this error must be dug up and cast out and the mind utterly freed from its demoralizing and stultifying influence. You can get nowhere while any of it remains a part of its consciousness. Until fully cleansed it is wholly impossible to accomplish the real work you came here to do. So you have been little by little freeing the mind from these untruths until now, with the help. of these teachings, it has- come to a realization of its being but a reflection, a part of your divine Consciousness, and it is willing to give up and let You take complete charge and do Your will in and through it.

Yes, it is willing to give up, even eager to do it. But it finds it cannot do it easily. Yet it sees that it must do it. And now listen, for here is -the vital part of this message:

Not until the mind not only does give up, but deliberately and consciously applies these truths here in the outer life, in all its thinking, speaking and acting, cleanses its consciousness of all error and turns its attention wholly to you within, seeing and knowing only the truth of its oneness with You, with Christ and with God,—can it be freed from its sense of separation, enter the kingdom and receive of its divine heritage,

IV. THE CRUCIFIXION

Paper # 37, Jan. 1932

We ask you to consider with us the last moments of Jesus' physical life and the last words He spoke on the cross.

While this was the crucifixion of our Saviour's mortal body, yet those who know realize that it was far more than that. Jesus came here not only to fulfill a prophecy, but to perform a mission and to be an example for all humanity to follow—to portray an ideal and at the same time be the way shower for all who are able to follow Him. And you must not forget that He knew from the beginning what the ending would be, knew that He would be crucified and yet He willingly and fearlessly gave Himself to His enemies.

To the world it seems the supreme sacrifice. And it was that, but in a different way from what the world understands. For if He is our Exemplar and Way-Shower then that means we and all men must go the way He went—even unto the crucifixion of our mortal selves.

But the world does not comprehend that, and could not believe it. It is only those who become His true disciples that understand, and they gladly go on to the end, even as He went, actually offering themselves to be crucified. For do they not know that self must be utterly destroyed; that it and it alone prevents the coming forth of the living Christ from the tomb of the mortal body?

Not let us go back to the cross. It is stated that Jesus' last words were, "It is finished," and then "He gave up the ghost." These, His words, and the ones following, are so significant that we want you to understand fully their hidden meaning.

Remember, Jesus being our Exemplar and Way-Shower, His life is the life we, His followers, must live. And we have shown how the Christ

63

must be born in our souls; must grow and thrive there and bring the outer Jesus part of us to maturity, which part must be taught by the Wise Men of the East" in preparation for our baptism in the Jordan, when the Holy Ghost, instead of descending on us as a dove, will actually as the Christ come forth from within us and take possession of our human personalities. From then on, He, the Christ of us, begins His mission of preaching and of calling to Him and teaching His disciples, but teaching chiefly His "beloved son," our human minds—which we will now liken to Jesus' human self with its mortal body (and which you must remember was what was crucified). For think you that Christ, the Son of God, Jesus' Higher Self, was not always guiding and teaching Jesus—even as your Higher Self He is ever guiding and teaching you?

The only difference between Him and us is that Jesus almost from His birth knew His Father in Heaven—-His Higher Self—as God Himself, and sought always to obey Him; and gas a result He was always able to receive direct from His Father's Consciousness whatever He needed to know. to have and to do. But with us there has been so much to unlearn and get -rid of first, and in many of us the birth of the Christ does not take place until maturity or later, and then there is so much teaching and preparation before He can get us ready for His use.

But this will give you an idea of what is going on and how it will gradually lead us to the crucifixion of self— the release from the sense of separation, the culmination and goal of the Christ Life on earth,

This brings us again to Jesus' words, "It is finished" If you who have received the baptism of the Holy Spirit and the Christ is now in possession (we know there are very few of such), and even if you who are aware of Him in your hearts, can conceive of the many- weary steps there are yet to take, carrying the cross of self, climbing the hill of Golgotha, and then being nailed on that cross, where you must suffer all that Jesus did, you can partially realize the agony of pain that Jesus endured.

For the consciousness of the flesh makes up the consciousness of the soul, yet Jesus' soul endured willingly, gladly, because He knew that so long as there was left in His human mind any consciousness that could feel pain or suffering, it was still separate in consciousness from its Higher Self, His Christ Consciousness, and was not ready for release and had not reached the goal of Oneness. Therefore, when Jesus said, "It is finished," He knew His. human mind had finally conquered, and it then gave up the ghost."

In other words, His mind fully realized that the body was an illusion, that the world without was an illusion, and they could hurt or hold its consciousness no longer; for it now knew it was pure Spirit, was conscious of its Divine Nature, of being always in the Consciousness of Divine Mind; it remembered then perfectly Whose mind it was and of What it was a part, even as the Christ of Jesus always knew. And if you will always remember that the Christ was the Higher Self of Jesus, even as the Christ within you the Comforter—is your Higher Self; it will make plain many things in Jesus life and His sayings that otherwise are impossible to understand.

When Jesus' mind had actually freed itself from its sense of separation and its consciousness was fully one with its Christ Consciousness, then you can see there could no longer be any consciousness of a physical body, anything to feel pain and anything to die. So it was but natural in the morning when they came to get His body, there was none there—it had dissolved and had disappeared from sight. For when we no longer hold in our consciousness a picture belief of a physical body and know such to be a false concept of our real body, which is pure Spirit, that picture of a physical body will disappear from our minds, which means from manifestation.

Remember the law: "Whatever we think and hold in our consciousness as being so, outmanifests itself;" and the obverse that when we stop believing a thing to be true and thus no longer feed it and keep it alive, it will disappear from our consciousness and consequently from physical expression; for it can then no longer exist. For all is consciousness, and what is no longer in consciousness naturally just is not.

So that when Jesus was finally able altogether to transcend the torture and agony as well as the mental effects of His bodily suffering, thus releasing His consciousness from it all, He knew He had conquered the 'Great Illusion" of separateness—had given up the ghost" of that belief, and of course then there was no longer a separate outer body—**its existence was** finished,-- there was now only His invisible and immortal soul body left.

But through the conquering and mastering of His body consciousness thus by His mind, He did not "die,' but consciously transcended His body consciousness, entering the higher vibration of His soul consciousness, apparently leaving His physical body behind. And because Of His leaving none of His consciousness in the body, there was no longer any life force to hold it together; so it just dissolved into the mental and etheric substance from which it had been created.

The fact that He thus mastered the idea of a physical body, wresting from it all power over His mind, indeed concluded or "finished" all need of a physical form. For His mind now being master of the idea, He could always by merely thinking and feeling himself again in a physical body cause the body to become visible, and He could thus manifest Himself in it at will, or He could dissolve it in His consciousness and it would instantly disappear. Why would that result? Because by transferring completely His center of consciousness from the idea of His physical body to the idea of His soul body, or vice versa, seeing and feeling Himself in either, He would be in either, as He wished; and on whatever plane of consciousness He was He would of course be visible to those on that plane.

For remember where His consciousness was, there He was; for His Consciousness is His soul, and He could now be conscious of being in His soul body or in His physical body at will, being fully master of the body idea. In other words, by focusing His thought upon either, He thus entered the consciousness either of the idea of His soul body or of His physical body, thereby raising or lowering His consciousness to the vibration of either, and becoming one with and therefore being in that body in which He wished to manifest, even as we have shown you is possible in the last few Papers.

This explains how Jesus was able to appear and disappear in the midst of His disciples before His ascension in His glorified body.

What do we mean by mastering an idea? Suppose you want to appear before a friend in New York and to deliver to him a message. That is an idea. If you could first see yourself •standing in front of your friend, and then could feel yourself there delivering to him your message, clearly seeing him hearing and receiving your words, you will catch our meaning. For just to the ex- tent that you are fully conscious of being there, having left behind all sense of everything else, will you have mastered that idea, and your friend, if psychic, will actually see you and hear you speak the words; or if he is at all sensitive he will feel or get the strong impression of your presence and of the words, almost as if he heard them.

Remember, everything is consciousness. You are an idea in consciousness. The above is an idea in consciousness. Every idea that is, is in consciousness. But there are many different planes of expression in consciousness, each having its own rate of vibration or wave length, and everything on a particular plane being visible to all else there, when contacted.

But every idea has- also its own individual vibration and all you have to do to contact any particular idea is to tune into its vibration and in a way you instantly become one with that idea. When Jesus conceived the idea of wanting to be with His disciples, He simply entered the consciousness of His old physical body idea; that is, He saw and felt Himself in it among them again, or in other words He tuned into that idea's vibration, and He was there. When He wanted to leave them He just withdrew His consciousness from the idea, and instantly He disappeared and was back again in His soul body on the soul plane.

THE SPIRITUAL SIGNIFICANCE

The spiritual significance of this all is that Jesus' mind had mastered its consciousness so that He could by thinking raise or lower it to whatever plane He wished, in order to connect up with the consciousness of any particular idea on that plane. By thus connecting up with an idea He became one with its consciousness and could either enter the idea and express through it or could receive from the idea anything about it He wished to know.

Remember the idea of a thing is the soul of that thing, as taught in "*The Impersonal Life*;' and the soul of anything is the consciousness which animates and constitutes its nature. Therefore when you master an idea, you master its, consciousness, and thus can compel it - to serve you in any way you will.

And of course as disciples and followers of Jesus, intending to follow Him unto the end, even unto the crucifixion of the mortal self, its burial and the resurrection from the tomb of matter, we must necessarily learn to master perfectly the ideas of self, of separation and of mortal flesh.

Only by studying carefully Jesus' life and teachings and faithfully patterning our lives after His, can we hope to accomplish what He did. But fear not that you cannot accomplish all that He accomplished, for did He not promise that all these things and even greater we would do, now that He has shown us the way? And remember we have within us the same power—that of the Holy Spirit—which enabled Him to meet and conquer in all of His trials and testings. And because He conquered so can we, for He promised also that the Father will enable us to do all things, as we push forward fearlessly, trusting Him perfectly at all times and under all circumstances.

You will note that we make a very careful distinction between Jesus and his human mind, and also between Jesus and the Christ, his Higher Self. Until you clearly perceive the Treason for and meaning of this distinction, you cannot understand the deep truths we have tried to convey.

It is our minds that must be required to do all those things that Jesus did, if we would follow Him. It is our minds that must give up -all this sense of self and of separation. It is the Jesus part of souls who know— which must require it, So that our minds of their own free will, will gladly and actually give up their consciousness and unite it with our soul consciousness, which is now one with our Christ Consciousness.

Now see if you can get this: It was the Christ who within Jesus was the inspirer and directer of all that Jesus said and did. It was He Who spoke in that highly significant way when saying, "*I am the way, the truth and the life; no man cometh unto the Father but by me."*

He was the Holy Spirit in Jesus, the Son of God.

It was the soul of Jesus that was the vehicle or abiding place of the Christ Spirit, making Him the purified man whom the world saw and knew as Jesus, and whom Jesus Himself called the Son of Man.

And then there was the mind of Jesus, which had been so perfectly trained and disciplined and consequently so cleansed and purified of self that there resulted a perfect co-operation of its consciousness with that of the soul, permitting the Christ within to do the Father's will on earth even as in Heaven, and thereby manifesting in Jesus' human personality the perfect "image and likeness" of the Father which He had created in the beginning.

But the Christ, Jesus, and the human mind and personality were really one, for they were but the consciousness of God manifesting now freely for the first time through a perfected channel containing no limitations whatever. The crucifixion was but the final and conclusive proof for all the world to see and recognize that God's Spirit had visited the earth in all the fullness of Its Splendor in human form, and had left with us Its Light until the end of time which would light the way for all of God's children so that they could know how to -return to Him, even as Jesus had returned.

In the above, hidden beneath the words, are given some very definite and vital instructions. Those of you who are ready will perceive them and will strive to prove them, and will thus become prepared and enabled to go through the crucifixion when you are "betrayed" by the Judas faculty of your nature. But remember that that very Judas faculty is employed by the Christ of you to deliver self over to your Initiators.

What follows will prove if you have fully attained the mastery of mind over matter, thereby enabling it to rise out of its "ghost" (the illusion of separateness) into its true consciousness, and become one with Jesus and all your Brothers in Spirit—a risen Christ.

THE SOUL LIFE OF A DISCIPLE

Here is another illuminating letter from our friend of the "Garden of the Soul." Dear Friends :

"It is truly glorious to know that we as our Higher Selves are-Sons of-God, having descendeth to earth—willingly and gladly under Christ's leadership to do our work of redemption. What a joy! In my realization of this I am so conscious of having taken possession of my soul— of being my Higher and Real Self, living in God's consciousness, where we are all so happy, where we have no desire for anything, for we have and are everything —all. I do not seem to be conscious of seeing a thing that is in manifestation; rather I seem to know I am the manifestation as well as the manifestor—or am as God Himself, and of course I just have and am everything— eternally.

'To look at my outer conditions would seem to deny this great truth, but I'm- not abiding in the outer appearances; they cannot touch me— I'm a Son of God abiding in my real home in a consciousness of perfect peace where there is no inharmony, disease, lack or limitation. These do not exist there, nor do they exist anywhere. For all that is, is God.

"Would there were words that could describe my garden now. I wish every one could share it with me.

It could not be recognized as the same garden I described to you some months ago. It is a thousand times lovelier than the loveliest garden you 've ever seen in the outer world; the flowers, so superbly perfect and beautiful, radiating love and trust as they happily give of their heavenly perfume! Won't you come into my garden? All ye that are weary and heavy laden—won't you come? There is peace here, and God's voice can easily be heard —maybe through the rustle of the leaves. Listen! It might be through the rippling of the brook, or when yon robin speaks to you. Look! The flowers give you nods of greeting, welcoming you into God's dwelling place, You are welcome—everyone. Won't you come in and abide in Me?

"1 shall be glad to relate my meeting with you on the soul plane that I mentioned in my last letter. I was walking with several women; I do not know where we were going, but we were laughing and chatting quite happily. In the distance we saw a small group of men coming towards us.

We knew they were from a very high plane because of the light they radiated. We commented on that and were quite eager to meet them.

When we met; quite- all spoke. Then you stepped up to me and began talking. It might seem odd that I knew you instantly, but it wasn't to me then. It was the most natural thing in the world that we knew each other we are like that on the soul plane.

'You talked with me about things in the Papers that ' were not quite clear to me, and you did it without my asking a single question -- you just seemed to know. As we were talking the others went on their way. When we finished we very casually did likewise. It was most helpful to me and I deemed it a privilege to talk with a Brother from such a high plane.

"Since then, however, a group of us from the earth plane (and I believe we are all students of the Sun Papers) have assembled many times in a temple-like building, and are being taught as well -as being given very definite instructions about our work. You are one of the Teachers or Brothers of Light who -are instructing us.

'I was quite familiar with parts of the last Paper before it was sent me, and was surprised when I read it to find it what had been taught in the Temple on the soul plane. I am very grateful to know all this; it is so helpful.

"This is how I 'got it': First I became conscious of being on a higher plane and in this Temple; then, I was conscious of only a few souls there. Later, however, I saw all the crowd of us. Presently I knew I was being taught some wonderful truths, though at first I knew not what they were; then I became conscious of you Brothers teaching us. The vibrations were wonderful, like soft music; then little by little that part of your Paper on 'Bringing the Kingdom down to earth' unfolded to me. It was marvelous having received it first from there.

"There is such a difference in being taught from the soul plane than being taught on the material plane. Everything there is truth and we feel so at one with every thing that is being said, and oh, everything is so different; there we know, while here we are hampered learners, struggling with ignorance. So naturally when I read it all in the Paper I was, very happy to know I had already received the instructions.

'Regarding the Paper previous to this one and that article on 'Vibrations,' well, an entirely different group or kind of Brothers, taught that. Such power they had!

They were Oriental looking, yet they were advanced souls. They just seemed strange to me because they were different from the ones I am used to contacting. What they taught is becoming very clear and practical to me. They were marvelous souls. "

In our reply to her we told her she had truly entered the Kingdom consciousness and had learned of its wonderful reality; that all in the without is pure illusion and exists only in the "separate" mortal mind as distorted concepts of such reality.

The beautiful appearance of her "garden" was because of the kind and loving thoughts, words and acts she had been sowing for so long and which had now grown and thrived under her loving care until all were in full bloom.

You must remember she sees these things in broad daylight not in sleep and not strictly as visions; for she is actually conscious of living on the soul plane and the physical plane simultaneously that is, while going about her daily activities she sees with her inner eyes another world of activity in the soul realm that is not separate from but is intimately related to her life and its problems in the outer world.

The meeting on the soul plane that she -described was most interesting and was not at all improbable, for you must realize that our real life is in the soul realm and that the physical is but a sorry reflection of the perfect life there of all disciples of Christ. So what was more natural than that there should be such •a meeting and discussing of the truths that are the most important things in our life there, even as here— that and the spreading of those truths and the teaching of them to our younger brothers.

What is also more natural than that all earnest students of the Sun Papers should meet regularly on the soul plane and receive the teachings there before they come to them on the outer plane? Remember all things take place first in the inner planes of being before they manifest on the outer; which accounts for the prophetic dreams and visions coming to many people before the things seen actually happen in the outer. It also accounts for many of our students writing us that somehow they seemed to have gotten what was in the Papers before they arrived, or that the deep truths they contained seemed not to be new when read the first time.

The explanation of our knowing each other, although neither had previously seen the other in the physical, is that we have had much correspondence, and long ago had learned to know each others' vibrations. And as on the soul plane one unconsciously puts one's soul vibrations into everything one gives out or expresses and cannot hide them, it is but natural that our souls had long since learned to know each other and had become well acquainted; even if her brain mind had never registered the fact of a previous meeting such as she was this time permitted to see.

Try to realize that you are always engaged in your true vocation on the soul plane, and if a student's chief thought is to find the Kingdom, then he is ever helped by Brothers of Light to find it, and goes to the schools where all he is capable of receiving is taught him. This is the case on all the different planes of consciousness of the soul realms, even as it is in the physical world. For as all the different grades in our public schools, colleges and universities represent and are intended to teach those on different planes of consciousness, so is it in the soul realms, although there each plane is apart and separate, as if in a different city or country.

On the lower planes there are always Brothers of Light from the higher planes teaching and helping those seeking the light; and then in whatever - vocation one -is engaged in the soul realms all seem to be ideal vocations, what one is doing in the physical being but an imperfect and sadly limited reflection of such vocation —one is doing his work happily and contentedly, because of the fancied ideal conditions surrounding him. For you must remember deep down in the soul of every worker on the physical plane there is the desire to be able to do all things perfectly, and the longing to have the perfect conditions exist which somehow he knows should be. It is so because, according to his degree of unfoldment, on whatever soul plane he is, he is there doing it perfectly as he conceives it, and in what he considers ideal conditions; and the soul is ever trying to prepare and develop the human mind so that it—the soul or real man—can bring forth into perfect expression man's real work and in such ideal conditions as are possible on the physical plane.

Try to realize that on the soul planes a soul is limited in his comprehension in the same degree as he is on the physical plane, for the human mind is but an outer extension of the soul's consciousness; but the comprehension pertains to and is concerned with what is expressing on the particular soul plane. There it is perfect, according to the degree of spiritual unfoldment of the consciousness of that plane, but the outer is a distorted reflection of such necessarily limited "perfection.'

Let us illustrate. As a child your estimate of certain things being ideal and perfect, as held before you went to school, would be greatly changed after you had been in school a few years and had gained wider knowledge of those and other things. Again high school knowledge would change your ideas about many of the things you admired and longed for when younger. And many of you remember how as a senior in college you looked down upon your freshman ideas and ideals.

Thus . would your ideals be ever changing, expanding and unfolding, and at each stage of spiritual growth would you gradually advance in your soul life to a higher plane of consciousness; for always on that plane would there be an ideal that would lead you on to the attainment of the perfection glimpsed. And so on to the highest soul plane the first realm of the Kingdom.

This highest soul plane, the plane of truly perfect forms, where the highest ideals are out-pictured in forms of superlative beauty, quality and perfection, is therefore called the causal plane, and it is the first stage of outmanifestation in which a sense of separation in consciousness is felt. For here the mind first builds its mental pictures as outer expressions of the ideas perceived in its Spiritual or Christ Consciousness in. its effort to understand and enjoy more fully those ideas. You might say that the causal plane is the manifest plane of the Kingdom or Christ Consciousness; while the unmanifest planes are those higher realms of consciousness where only pure ideas exist and there is no need for forms or pictures.

More will be given about the inner planes of being and especially the Kingdom in later Papers, for it is our desire that our students become so acquainted with their soul home in the inner world that when the great change comes it will be a natural and easy transference of their centers of consciousness. In fact we hope to enable many to enter the consciousness of the real world at will before the change takes place.

V. LAZARUS, COME FORTH!

Paper #38, Feb. 1932

When Jesus was sent word by Mary and Martha that their brother Lazarus, whom Jesus loved, was sick, He said to His disciples:

"This sickness is not unto death, but for the glory of God, that the Son of God might be glorified thereby."

Then He stayed two days in the place where He was with His disciples before going to see Lazarus. In the meantime Lazarus died, and as Jerusalem was fifteen furlongs, away, when they reached there he had been in his grave four days.

Evidently Jesus knew this, for He said to His disciples: "Our friend Lazarus sleepeth; but I go that I may awake him out of sleep." The disciples thought that he meant it was just ordinary sleep.

From Jesus' first statement it is apparent that He purposely let Lazarus die, for He wanted by means of this experience to teach His disciples as well as Mary and Martha and all who afterwards* learned of it a great lesson, and we will try to point out that lesson to you.

"When Martha heard that Jesus was coming, she went and met Him, but Mary stayed in the house.

"Then said Martha unto Jesus, Lord, if thou hadst been here, my brother had not died. But I know that even now, whatsoever thou wilt ask of God, God will- give it thee.

'Jesus said unto her, Thy brother will rise again. "Martha saith unto him, I know that he shall rise again in the resurrection at the last day.

'Jesus said unto her, I am the resurrection and the life; he that believeth in me, though he were dead, yet shall he live; and whosoever liveth and believeth in me shall never die. Believest thou this?

"She said unto him, Yea Lord, I believe that thou art the Christ, the Son of God, which should come unto the world. '

In every one of us there are the Mary and Martha qualities—the Mary quality that sits at home and mourns and condemns when someone or something dear has been taken away from us; and the Martha quality that goes to seek the Lord, knowing that by prayer and asking God everything will be made right again.

There is also that in every one of us which hears such prayers and, if we listen carefully, it will say, "I am the resurrection and the life; he that believeth in me, though he were dead, yet shall he live. And he that liveth and believeth in me shall never die. Believeth thou this?"

The Higher Self, the Comforter, the Christ within, ever says this to His disciples, to those who love Him and turn to Him in their sorrow and need. For is He not their life, their health, their strength everything that they are? He is -their Real Self, the real Spirit animating their bodies, their minds and their souls. They are nothing without Him—are in a way dead, or as Jesus said of Lazarus, are sleeping, and He -alone can awaken them.

You, who think you have found the Christ, hear these His words and **believe; for He is the resurrection and** the life, and if you live in Him and believe in Him, you will never die. We will prove this to you later.

When Jesus came to Lazarus' grave which was a cave, and a stone lay upon it, He said,

'Take ye away the stone.

'But Martha said unto Him, Lord, by this time he stinketh; for he hath been dead four days.

'Jesus saith unto her, Said I not unto thee that if thou wouldst believe, thou shouldst see the glory of God?

After they had taken away, the stone, Jesus lifted up His eyes and said,

"Father, I thank thee that thou hast heard me. And I know that thou hearest me always; but because of the people which stand by I said it, that they may believe that thou hast sent me.

"And when he thus had spoken, he cried with a loud voice, Lazarus, come forth.

"And he that was dead came forth, bound hand and foot with grave clothes; and his face was bound about with a napkin. Jesus saith unto them, Loose him, and let him go." (The foregoing quotations from the 11th chapter of St. John).

Everyone is weighted down with the stone of belief that he has to die, and before anything -can be done for him that stone must be taken away.

But even the Martha quality in us hesitates to believe that death can be conquered; that lie is so old that it stinks in the consciousness, poisoning even our faith and trust in God.

But the Christ, our Real Self, who knows, ever repeats, "If thou believest that I alone am, and that this body of flesh is only the garment I put on and off at will, thou shalt see the glory of God.'

With the lie about having to die -removed from our consciousness— a stone that has weighted us to the earth for ages our purified and uplifted minds can say in the freedom of the new vision that is then ours,

"Father, I thank Thee that Thou hast heard me; and I know that Thou hearest me always; for Thou knowest the inmost desires of my heart, even inspiring in me such desires. But before I was dumb, for I did not understand; but now I know that whatever Thou inspirest me to do, that can I do, for it is Thy purpose to do it through me."

And likewise did Jesus offer a prayer to His Father-in-Heaven, His Higher Self, thanking Him for that which was to be done through His agency; this being chiefly to impress those who stood by that they might learn that God was working through Him.

For think you that Jesus did not know that Lazarus was not dead, but that he was really sleeping? Think you that through His uplifted consciousness He could not see the soul of Lazarus just as he was at that moment in the real world of the soul; could not see Lazarus sleeping there after his transition, as is the case with most souls after four days, giving them time to regain their strength after the depletion of their vital forces caused by sickness? Remember, all this sickness and death was only a belief of the old mortal consciousness, and sleep was the means whereby it would be freed from the effects of such devitalizing belief.

Of course Jesus knew all this and could see Lazarus just as he was in the inner realm of being, invisible to all eyes but His. Because of the deep sleep into which Lazarus' soul had fallen, Jesus, in order to awaken him, called to him with a loud voice,

"Lazarus, come forth!"

But Jesus did something more than call to him, for He also knew where Lazarus' spirit was. Even as when our physical bodies sleep, our souls retire within to our homes in the soul realm, so when our souls sleep do our spirits retire within to their homes in the spiritual realms. Jesus had first to recall Lazarus' spirit back into his soul body, and thus awaken his soul, and then He had to recall his spirit and soul back into his physical body.

However Jesus knew He could not do the latter without the Father's aid, but with His assistance, which He knew would be given Him, He could do anything—for had not the Father inspired Him to do all -that He was doing? He confidently called to Lazarus to come forth, knowing that the Father deep within Lazarus' spirit would hear and empower Lazarus to transcend the law of matter or of mortal mind, rise out of his soul sleep, once more enter the idea of his body consciousness and thus revivify his old fleshly garment.

This actually resulted in response to Jesus' call. Lazarus rose up out of the grave in which his body had been lying, came forth with all his grave clothes still around him, and his face wrapped with a napkin. These wrappings symbolized the old beliefs that still enfolded him in his mortal consciousness.

So the. Christ of us must command all our faculties to "loose him and let him go' '—to loose the mind of these lies and let it be free to know the truth that there is no real death. The soul can never die, for it houses the spirit; it can sleep; it can withdraw from the brain mind; but as the soul is our consciousness it will always exist, whether in a physical body or out of it.

The lesson Jesus sought to teach was that the flesh and even the brain mind were of no importance and had no power, only as the I Am, the Christ, endued them with power and gave them their life. Jesus let Lazarus die in order that He could teach the world, to the glory of God, that the Christ Spirit, the Real Man, a Son of God, is _superior to all limitations of the flesh and of the mind responsible for it, and even to death itself; and that when anyone knows his Sonship, his Christ nature, he can command his soul, and through the grace of God, his soul, or his consciousness, will come forth from its sleep, re-enter the body and rise out of the grave of its old mortal beliefs and be free hereafter to live its true soul life.

You will note that in these words we have given you the personal application and have shown what you can do in the raising and freeing of your own soul, as well as that of another—when you are in your true consciousness as a Son of God, as was Jesus, and which we have taught you how to enter.

This proves that in that consciousness you are the resurrection and the life, that you are always the risen life from which soul and body consciousness derive all their sustenance; and that when you can get your mind to come "up" of its own free will and live in your consciousness, it can never die, nor can its outer expression, the body; for even it then has no sense of separation, but is also partaking of and abiding in your consciousness, which being God's consciousness is the only consciousness.

But this also shows how you can in that same consciousness see, even as Jesus saw, that one recently de ceased no longer than four days, can be similarly awakened and recalled to physical life,—providing that your mind has the same absolute trust in God, the same sense of oneness with Him as had Jesus, and which is the natural consciousness of every Christed soul.

Read the above over many times and ponder it well.

There is so much of vital moment in it all that we urge every disciple to stay with it, day after day, until all its wonderful meaning becomes clear and a living part 01 your consciousness. When this is accomplished we promise that some remarkable things will happen to you.

THE TIME OF TRIBULATION

In the foregoing article and the one-on—the -Crucifixion, we have pointed you to some very great truths, and we have explained their operation sufficiently so that all who are ready to make the sacrifice of self can use these truths to free themselves from the darkness, confusion and suffering now manifesting everywhere in the world, and which before they are removed will grow many times worse.

Where have we been leading you? To the Kingdom? Why? Not just to free you from the results of your own sins and those of the world, but that you may know the truth and receive your divine heritage as a Son of God; and then will turn about and use your human instrument to help us and all our Brothers in Christ to lead as many others as possible out of the darkness into the Light.

You in your human self are nothing, but as a soul awakening into the consciousness of your true being and thus becoming another channel through which the Light can be poured for the freeing of the world, are of very great importance are the most valuable help you can be to God and to His army of Light.

The time is growing very short. The great battle is on in the inner realms. Can you not see the strenuous and unceasing warfare for the souls of men that is now being waged everywhere? Everyone is being tested tempted as never before in the history of the world. Every possible pressure is being brought to bear upon men's minds day and night by the forces of darkness—every p thing that can tempt and lure them away from the teachings of their parents, from the following of their higher instincts, and from their love of goodness and purity.

Need we point you to the agencies being used, to the newspapers giving their front pages and scareheads to murderers, notorious gangsters and criminals and their activities; to the jazz types of- music; to the cubist and futurist trends in art and architecture; to the wide-spread drinking and bootlegging and all their accompanying evils; to the movies and theaters specializing in underworld, racketeer and sex plays; to the magazines following in line, with scores of new cheap ones being devoted entirely to such subjects?

Constantly through these agencies are suggestions being poured into the minds of the people, and unconsciously almost all are finding themselves being pushed into doing things which, if they stopped and reasoned it out, they would never of themselves think of doing.

Do you realize that ninety per cent of the people believe whatever they read in the newspapers and national magazines, and it does not occur to them to think and reason about whether it is all so or not; or if they did they would have no cause for believing differently, for they have no other source of information all sources being wholly controlled and directed by these super-forces to give out the information that they want the people to believe—and no more?

And do you realize that most people are naturally credulous and trusting and wish to believe what they are told? They refuse to consider that they are being deliberately deceived by evil powers that are seeking to further their own sinister ends.

Think you there is no actual direction back of all this that it merely happens, that men are just naturally drifting into a state where they are forgetting all about God and losing their faith in an invisible Deity, discarding all the teachings of their forefathers?

If so, recall the methods now being used in Russia at the present time to mould the minds of the people, especially of the children in their schools, who are taught that God is but a myth, a belief of the unintelligent foisted upon humanity by the capitalists; and the new generation there is actually growing to maturity in a world which to them has no God.

Can you not see that no mere group of men is doing this that there is a powerful and invisible intelligence with a most diabolic and far-reaching purpose back of it all, and which is just as surely working from the inner planes of being, influencing and weakening all minds in which selfishness in any way rules, as is the Christ Spirit influencing and strengthening all in which a loving desire to help others is dominant?

Be not deceived, you followers of Christ, but keep your eyes wide open, for these are the days prophesied by our beloved Leader, Christ Jesus, in the 24th chapter of Matthew. Read carefully the whole chapter, but note particularly these verses.

"For many shall come in my name, saying I am Christ, and shall deceive many.

"And ye shall hear of wars and rumors of wars: see that ye be not troubled; for all these things MUST come to pass, but the end is not yet.

"For nation shall rise against nation and kingdom against kingdom; and there shall be famines and pestilences and earthquakes, in divers places. "All these are the beginning of sorrows.

'Then shall they deliver you up to be afflicted and shall kill you; and ye shall be hated of all nations for my name's sake.

"And then shall many be offended, and shall betray one another, and shall hate one another.

"And many false prophets shall arise, and shall deceive many.

'And because iniquity shall abound, the love of many shall wax cold.

'But he that shall .endure to the end, the same shall be saved.

"And this gospel of the Kingdom shall be preached in all the world for a witness unto all nations; and then shall the end come.

When ye therefore shall see the abomination of desolation, spoken of by Daniel the prophet, stand in the holy place (whoso readeth, let him understand) ;

"Then let them which be in Judea flee into the mountains . For there shall be great tribulation, such as was not from the beginning of the world to this time, no nor ever shall be.

"And except those days shall be shortened, there shall no flesh be saved; but for the elect's sake those days shall be shortened.

'Then if any man shall say unto you, 10, here is Christ, or there; believe him not.

'For there shall arise false Christs, and false prophets, and shall show great signs and wonders; insomuch that, if it were possible, they shall deceive the very elect.

"Behold, I have told you before.'

We have printed in heavy type the statements to which we wish you to pay particular attention. We especially want you to note that we seem to be living in the days about which Jesus was prophesying. It is true that many times in history have there been those who claimed those particular times were meant. But we are now facing a period when the whole world is involved in the conditions mentioned, when previously only a few countries or at most one continent were affected.

We are now in the midst of wars and rumors of war. 'These things must come to pass." Can anyone deny it, or see how war can be avoided, with the mad scramble to increase armaments going on in every nation in their anxiety to be prepared for what they all expect to come? But the end is not yet. "These are but the beginning of sorrows.

Therefore, watch that they do not "deliver you up to be afflicted." That -is, be prepared, so that in His Name (in His Consciousness) you can rise above it all and be free and untouched by whatever comes to pass.

Many are beginning to come and pose as Christs, to speak and prophesy in His Name and to "show great signs and wonders,' so that they are deceiving all but the elect. See that you are not caught by such. Remember, you have always within you a sure Guide and Authority, Who if you will turn to Him will instantly point out to you the fallacies in their speech and the qualities in their personalities that are not of Christ, and Who will surely prevent your being deceived.

You can easily see that iniquity is . abounding everywhere, especially in high places, and it is not to be wondered at that love and faith in God should "wax cold" when national authority prevents the word Christ being used in any state document, when the words Christ and Christian are eliminated from every school book in America, and when no President of the United States has dared to take his inaugural oath on the open pages of the New Testament.

Think you that the Anti-Christ is not almost in complete control of the outer world, which means has almost complete control of men's minds of all but those who have been tested and proven in their allegiance to Christ? It is the testing and the proving that is now going on in the battling for men's souls by the forces of evil and of righteousness, each side striving to win and hold those whom they can reach and influence. And it is only those who have definitely chosen Christ and who "endure to the end" that will be saved.

The Gospel of the Kingdom is now being preached to all the world. It is the witness, pointing the way for all men and calling upon them to repent; for the Kingdom of God is truly at hand, is closer than even many of the elect dream. Every people on the earth has been reached and invited to come into His Kingdom. So now we are ready for the end. We have told all men the truth, we have uncovered to them the evil. They now must decide whom they will serve. No one can do that for them. And then they must be tested and proven. All can be saved, if they will endure in the truth.

But evil has cajoled, coerced and so deceived the minds of men that few will endure; vast numbers of them have succumbed to evil, have been enticed by it over to the side of darkness, and now evil sits on the throne and has become the king of the world. It only remains for it to become established in the holy places, compelling all the nations of the world to repudiate Christ and God as they have done in Russia, and then will the abomination of desolation begin, spoken of by Daniel and Jesus.

Then is the time when all disciples of Christ must flee into the mountains of the Spirit, must deliberately and actually transcend their body consciousness and enter and abide in their Christ Consciousness.

Those who are journeying with us have been taught to do this. Every stage of the process has been shown them and been made so plain that all may know. Only those whose minds have been more engrossed in outer things and would not be convinced of the necessity of doing what we persistently urged, have failed to find the Kingdom, and are now unhappy and discouraged; and unless they deliberately go back and start over again and study and live with the teachings until they prove their truths every step of the way, they will find when the evil days come that they will have no place to flee. "For in those days there shall be great tribulations, such as was not from the beginning of the world to this time, no nor ever shall be."

We have spoken of these things in our booklet "Brother hood, ' published in 1927, but in the Papers only casually. But the time has come when we must needs speak plainly and tell all our dear ones of the vital necessity of thoroughly preparing themselves, of now applying assiduously the teachings given to the immediate problems before them until all are fully proven; so that they will be ready for whatever comes. You can now see one of the chief things we have been preparing you for; we have been so insistent in urging you to discipline and master your minds only in order that they learn instantly and perfectly to obey when you command.

We want not one of you to be left behind. But that means that those who have not been diligent in their study and efforts begin now as never before to make the finding of the Kingdom and the living in their Christ Consciousness first in all their thinking, speaking and acting. For as stated by the Master, although the time of tribulation will be shortened, yet will there be but few in the flesh saved.

He speaks of the "elect" they who cannot be deceived. Would you be one of them? Then you must find Him within your hearts and learn to retire within to the soul realm and to abide there with Him. He in those days will be your only refuge and strength.

With those who are able thus to retire within—to "flee into the mountains,' it matters not what happens to their garments of flesh. For they will then be consciously living in their immortal soul bodies in a higher dimension that will soon manifest upon the earth.

Those who will endure to the end are those who have passed the tests in this term of earth's schooling, called the Piscean Age, and have graduated into the Aquarian, the next higher grade. It means that they will have faithfully learned the lessons taught them by their great Teacher, have freed their minds from all the error and sins of mortal consciousness, so that they will have risen into His Consciousness and thereby will have earned the right to follow and be with Him in the higher grade.

It also means that their minds having been cleansed of all the old beliefs of mortality, including the sense of separation and the fear of death, their bodies will no longer be really flesh, but the light of the Spirit will shine through them making their youthful and immortal soul bodies within visible to those who have eyes to see. In other words, the Word, the Christ of them, will actually have become the flesh.

So it makes no difference to them in the terrible times that will later manifest in the outer, what becomes of their physical bodies. They will merely withdraw their consciousness from the body and it will no longer be visible, for the physical is not the real body; it exists in the Soul realm. But when they so choose they can again appear in the physical wherever they wish to be.

What really will take place is that on account of the near presence of the great Army of Light on the inner plane of being, its vibrations of Divine Love are so powerful that the whole earth and everyone on it will be affected in their inner nature in such a way that everything not attuned to the Christ Consciousness will be unable to endure its high vibrations and will consequently disappear from manifestation.

The fact is, these new vibrations are going to be those continually manifesting in the New Age, or in the higher grade of earth's school into which those who have passed the tests and endured to the end will have graduated.

We want you to realize all that this means. First try to understand that this great Army of Light is composed of all the souls of heaven and earth who have entered the Christ Consciousness. This means that you, if you are a disciple of Christ, in your soul consciousness are of this army, for being conscious of serving Him in your heart, which means in your soul consciousness, your soul is definitely enlisted with Him and His Light is guiding you in all that you do. And many new recruits are joining this army on the inner plane daily, due to the increasing efforts of all workers on both the outer and inner planes.

Then try to realize that this great army of souls comprises the actual inhabitants of the Kingdom of Heaven, and they are bringing with them the Light of Heaven, which means of their Christ Consciousness, right down upon- the earth; and that their powerful Light will drive out all darkness of error and evil from mens minds, go that there will be no longer any mortal bodies, for all sense of separation—of there being a body and a soul— will have disappeared; there will then be only the soul and its body.

Can you not then see that all who cannot rise into their Christ Consciousness while undergoing the tribulations of the testing period will be unable to endure its high vibrations, and will naturally give up their fleshly garments in one way or another and retire back into their soul homes on whatever planes they happen to be?

Then naturally the disciples of Christ will possess the earth, bringing Heaven, their real world, where their souls dwell, where all is goodness and perfection, down into actual manifestation upon the earth, and which world will then be visible to all those belonging and dwelling on the earth. While all those in the lower grades of the Spirit who were formerly their comrades on earth will be invisible, but will still be alive and visible to one another, each on their respective soul planes, exactly as it is now on the various inner planes of the soul. But we will explain more about this in the next Paper.

VI. THE SON OF MAN

Paper #39, March 1932.

"Immediately after the tribulation of those days shall the sun be darkened, and the moon shall not give her light, and the stars shall fall from' heaven, and the powers of the heavens shall be shaken :

"And then shall appear the sign of the Son of Man in heaven; and then shall all the tribes of the earth mourn, and they shall see the Son of Man coming in the clouds of heaven with power and great glory.

And he shall send his angels with a great sound of a trumpet, and they shall gather together his elect from the four winds, from the one end of heaven to the other. " ——Mathew 24: 29-31.

In view of what was stated in the previous Paper about the tribulations of the present time being the ones referred to by Jesus and quoted from an earlier part of the same chapter of Matthew, we wish now to consider His words above.

We will first point you to what He says in the 34th and 35th verses

following:

"Verily I say unto you, This generation (meaning this age, for we know it did not take place in the generation succeeding Jesus) shall not

pass, till all these things be fulfilled.

"Heaven and earth shall pass away, by my words shall not pass away."

Remember, these are Jesus' actual words; they are His promises very solemnly impressed upon His disciples, and we cannot but accept that they will come true.

We will assume therefore that these days of tribulation through which we are passing are the last days to which He referred, which except they be shortened there will be no flesh saved. But we know they will be shortened for the elect's sake, and we will also assume that the elect— His true disciples now on earth—are fleeing to the "mountains" of the Spirit and will abide . there and await the appearance the sign of the - Son of Man in heaven.

Before this sign appears, He says that the sun and moon will be darkened and the stars -from heaven and the powers of heaven will be shaken.

We will try to convey to you what this means, but first it will be necessary to tell you that what man sees with his mortal eyes and what appears to be the sun, moon and stars of the heavens, and also what seems to be the earth, are not what he understands them to be in his mortal mind. They are but symbols or his mental concepts of great realities that exists in the inner realms of Spirit—but not in the outer world of the physical.

We make this clearer in the article on "The One Mind" that follows herein, but we now ask you to consider that when rising into the Christ Consciousness (fleeing into the mountains) we leave the physical world altogether, and enter a realm where there are no sun, moon, stars or other "powers of the heavens;" all these will have passed away. The light of our own souls in that realm suffices.

Then what is more natural than to assume that after the tribulations are over and the "descent" of the Kingdom begins, the first thing to be noticed by all those still in mortal consciousness will be -the. unusual darkness caused by the seeming withdrawal of the light from all material sources, as well as the shaking or disruption of the supposed powers of the heavens.

Then in the darkness will appear the sign of the Son of Man in heaven. A great and wondrous light will appear, such as was never before seen upon earth, causing all men to lament, fearing they know not what. And then out of this light amidst the clouds of heaven will come forth the Son of Man with all the power and glory of His Kingdom about Him and surrounded by great hosts of, angels.

In other words, Jesus Christ, as the Son of Man, after causing His sign to appear, will send His angels with loud trumpeting to gather His elect from the four corners of the Kingdom, and they with the Great Beings and angels from the celestial realms will form the Great Army of Light spoken of in the preceding Paper, who will be seen in all their great power and glory bringing the light of heaven right down upon the earth.

When the Son of Man shall come in His glory, and all the holy angels with Him, then shall He sit upon the throne of His glory.

"And before Him shall be gathered all nations; and He shall separate them, one from another, as a shepherd divideth his sheep from the goats.

"And He shall sit the sheep on His right hand, but the goats on His left.

"And shall the King say unto them on His right hand, Come, ye blessed of -My Father, inherit the Kingdom prepared for you from the foundation of the world. .

"Then shall He -say also unto them on the left hand, Depart from Me, ye cursed, into everlasting fire, prepared for the devil and his angels.

"These shall go away into everlasting punishment; but the righteous into life eternal. "

We do not wish to speak now of the Lord's judgement of those that remain, but rather of the manner of His coming and what it means. In order to make clear to your understanding its true meaning, it will be necessary to quote some of Paul's statements regarding this great event, for he seems to have had a revelation concerning it.

He said, "Behold I show you a mystery (or secret) ; we shall not all sleep (or die) , but we shall all be changed, in the twinkling of an eye, at the last trump, for the trumpet shall sound, and the dead shall be raised incorruptible, and we shall be changed.' 1 Cor. 15: 5 1-2.

Also in I Thess., "But I would not have you to be ignorant, brethren, concerning them which are asleep (or are dead), that ye sorrow not, even as others which have no hope;

'For if we believe that Jesus died and rose again, even so them also .which sleep in Jesus (or who are in their Christ Consciousness on the soul plane, having discarded their mortal bodies; or died} will God bring with Him (with Jesus)

"For this we say unto you by the word of the Lord, that we which are alive and remain unto the coming of the Lord shall not prevent them which are asleep (or are dead) ;

' 'For the Lord Himself shall descend from heaven with a shout, with the voice of the archangel, and with the trump of God; and the dead in Christ (those 'dead' but in their Christ Consciousness, where they have joined with Him on the soul plane) shall rise first.

"Then we, which are alive and remain, shall be caught up together with them in the clouds, to meet the Lord in the air; so shall we ever afterward be with the Lord." 1 Thess., 4 :13-17.

In other words, those of us conscious disciples of Christ who are still alive in the flesh will rise out of our mortal consciousness into our Christ Consciousness and shall be with them and the Lord therein ever afterward.

In reality, as shown in the preceding Paper, will that Consciousness then rule on earth, through our Lord, Jesus Christ, Who will sit upon the throne of His glory; and those of us who are in that Consciousness with Him will rule under Him and teach the nations the laws and principles of the Christ Life.

But what we would have you understand is   that not all who are alive will be in that Consciousness, for as Jesus says, there will then be gathered before Him all nations that are left,   and He shall separate them one from another, the sheep on His right hand, and the goats on His left.

To those on His right hand He will say, "Come, ye blessed of my Father, inherit the Kingdom prepared for you from the foundation of the world."

"For I was anhungered, and ye gave me meat; I was thirsty, and ye gave me drink; I was a stranger, and ye took me in:

'Naked, and ye clothed me; I was sick, and ye visited me; I was in prison, and ye came unto me

And then He explained that "Inasmuch as ye have done it unto one of the least of these my brethren, ye have done it unto me.'

Those on His right hand will be the "children" of the Kingdom, those, no matter what their religion, color or race, who believe in a Supreme Being and in their hearts worship and ever seek to please and serve Him by being kind and helpful to their fellows; or no matter how much they are deemed to be heathens, barbarians, unworthy or ignorant, by those looking to the priesthood for their authority. These we, their elder brothers, will teach the mysteries of Christ, which have been hidden through the ages from the wise, but then will be made plain, so that, all the world may know.

You can easily see that among all the peoples of the world, the "elect", the true disciples of Christ, are very few in number—and that they as elder brothers must be the leaders, the teachers, guides, helpers and protectors of the different nations of their younger brothers who will then be under their care. In a way many of us realize now our true mission in being here at this particular time, and are doing all we can to teach and prepare for the New Age those who come to us for light and help.

Many are coming into the light these days, as the truth is taught them and their former errors are uncovered and made plain, and they are repenting and aligning themselves on the side of Christ and of righteousness. These, if they endure unto the end, will be among those who are left after the tribulations, and who will sit on the right hand of the Lord.

Those who persist in their selfishness and unrighteousness, who rebel and refuse to acknowledge and obey the spirit of God in their hearts, and who are permitted to endure to the end, will be placed on the left hand of the Lord. "These shall go away into everlasting (or agelasting, or end of the age, according to the Greek text) punishment; but the righteous unto eternal (immortal)

In other words as stated in Rev. XX, they "lived not again until the thousand years had finished;" but the righteous will become immortal souls.

But what we wish you particularly to note is the distinction between the "elect", those already living in their Christ consciousness, and those who are their younger brothers and who will be under their care and guidance. We have told you how these children in Christ will gradually be brought by their elder brothers to the maturity of their Christ understanding until they too attain the full stature of Christ.

Of the elder brothers the same chapter of Revelation states, "Blessed and holy is he that hath part in the first resurrection (those who ascend at Christ's coming and meet Him in their Christ Consciousness); on them the second death (they no longer have anything to die) hath no power, but they shall be priests of God and Christ, and shall reign with Him a thousand years.'

You who are receiving these Impersonal teachings and who have learned to know the Christ in your hearts— the Comforter, and are waiting upon and serving Him there, are the children of the Kingdom and who, if you endure to the end or not, will be a part of the Kingdom of the New Age.

But you who have entered the Christ Consciousness and know your identity as a Son of God, your oneness with Christ and the Father, you are- of those who will have part in the first resurrection and will meet the Lord 'in the air" and will descend with Him to establish His Kingdom upon the earth.

Can you not now see what we have been preparing you for, helping all whose own Higher Selves were urging them to follow with us to the end—to the Kingdom which we all started out to reach?

This is the goal—to enable you consciously to enter the Kingdom, by way of the Christ Consciousness ("no man cometh unto the Father but by Me") so that you will be one of those to meet the Lord in the air (in that Consciousness) when He comes.

Some of you have entered that Consciousness and are more or less able to enter it at will and to abide in it for a time. Many of you are on the verge of entering, are passing through the cleansing fires of the tribulations and are having the last vestiges of self burned away— are actually going through your crucifixion. These earnest ones, if they endure to the end, will surely be saved, and we urge that you spend much of your time from now on in prayer, striving to hear and obey no voice but Christ's.

To those who have permitted doubts, discouragement and fear of failure, to enter the mind, because of no seeming evidence of attainment despite their earnest efforts, know that you are but succumbing to the enemy, who alone has instilled such thoughts into your minds in order to weaken and stop you. Will you yield thus to him, forgetting all the help, inspiration and proof of Him Whom you have been following and serving, when so near the goal? Can you not realize that this may be but the final test of your desire and determination to win the Kingdom?

The disciple is always tested and reached through the weakest part of his nature. The enemy knows just where that is and he always plays on that part until, if possible, he weakens the resistance of other parts and thereby demoralizes the mind and through it the will. Are you going to let him play with you in this way.

We give you this caution now, so that you may understand what it all means, and will carry on. Many of you are those who have never heard a definite voice, who have had no tangible evidence of an inner life or of actual guidance, or who all their lives. have fruitlessly longed for a glimpse of the Master's face and to feel His Presence. But hear what dear words of comfort Jesus says to such: "Blessed are they that have not seen, and yet have believed." it, and being one of those who will enter and dwell in it in the New Age.

So that it is really unimportant if -a disciple -wins -the Kingdom while in his physical body, or if he loses his physical body. For it is not his real body, and in the new conditions and higher vibrations that will manifest in the near future, his beautiful and perfect soul body will be the only one visible, and he will no longer have any use for the old physical body. Therefore halt not your efforts. It is not what you have experienced and is accredited by your human mind, but what you are in your heart, that counts. Just know that if your whole heart, mind and soul are set on finding the Kingdom , nothing in heaven, earth or hell can prevent your finding.

From what has been said, can you not see that the real meaning of those who endure to the end being the ones who be saved, does not refer to the saving of their physical bodies? For did not Jesus say, "Then shall they deliver you up to be afflicted and shall kill you?" Then it must refer to those who will endure to the end in a perfect faith and trust in God or in Christ, despite anything that may happen to them in the outer. They alone will be "saved" for the New Age. They are the "sheep", the steadfast ones whom none can deceive or destroy. Not meaning that all such will be killed, for all conscious disciples will be able to free themselves from their captors, even as did Jesus, Peter and Paul.—See Luke 4:30; John 8:59 and 10:39; Acts 12:6-11.

We might add that in this new and higher grade of the Aquarian Age when the Christ Consciousness will rule, it will be an exact reversal of present conditions. Then the heaven and the real world will be the only one visible on earth, while what is at present visible will become invisible, because of being on a lower vibration on another plane of consciousness.

Therefore, with Paul we say, "Beloved brethren, be ye steadfast, immovable, always abounding in the work of the Lord, for inasmuch as ye know that your labor is not in vain in the Lord."

"The Lord of peace himself give you peace always.

The Lord be with you all."

THE ONE MIND

The One Mind is everywhere.

If you can but know it, It is not only in the air, pressing up against your face, your arms, your body, but It is the intelligence holding the atoms of your body together.

It is also the consciousness of the cells of your body that knows just what to do to make every organ,- nerve or muscle, of which they are a part, function perfectly—if let alone; knows just. what to take from the blood what is needed to build bone, flesh, fat, nerves, tissue, hair, nails, etc.

It is likewise the intelligence directing the birth, growth, decay and death of all mineral, vegetable and animal life expression; directing also the actual existence of all inanimate objects, such as a chair, a house or an automobile, for did not the minds of men first conceive the ideas to build these objects, and did they not receive these ideas from the One Mind?

Think! This One Mind is not only in all men and all things, but contains all men and all things within Itself, explaining the meaning of Paul's statement that "In him we live, move and have our being," or that in God's Mind we and all things live, move and have our being.

You can easily understand this when you realize that in your mind your whole world and everything in it have their being—for your world is in fact composed only of your concepts, ideas or thought pictures of what you think are outside of you in the so-called physical world.

When in reality there is no actual physical world— that is only your mind's interpretation of the sources of the vibrations continually reported to you by your five senses. The real things you see, hear, feel, etc., are the concepts, -ideas -and- have formed in your mind of what you think exist outside of your particular center of consciousness and which live, move and have their being only in the world of your mind; even as we and all, things in the reality of our perfect being exist in God's Mind.

We recite all this in order to show you that all is Mind, that everything is operating -in Mind, and in Mind only. And therefore Mind being everywhere and of knowing all things and hence being all powerful, because of its vast knowledge naturally it -must operate in perfect and continuous harmony. It could not be otherwise in such an all-wise and all perfect Mind.

Go over the above carefully and ponder on each sentence until its full meaning becomes clear in your mind, and it thus gets in harmony with the One Mind.

Do not try too hard at first to grasp the truth of the statement that in reality there is no actual physical world, for that will come to you later without effort—when the other truths are fully realized. But try to see how everything takes place first in mind—that it is always first an idea in some man's mind, coming forth into it from the One Mind, before it seemingly outmanifests in the so called physical world.

Then if you will turn back to our first two statements and grasp the fact that the One Mind is also in the air pressing up against your body and against all bodies, as well as is in all bodies, you can easily gee that what we call outmanifesting in the physical world is but a further coming forth of ideas out of man's mind into the outermost strata of mind, or into the visibility of material form; in the same way that they first come forth from the innermost of the One 'Mind into man's mind, and finally push through into the physical realm of being.

But man's mind being between the innermost and the outermost can easily, or should be able easily, to connect itself with either, by knowing its oneness with both through the realization that there is in actuality only ONE mind.

Through a perfect realization of this truth, it instantly becomes attuned to the One Mind, and is able perfectly to control the manifestation of its ideas in the outermost as well as to receive whatever ideas it needs from the innermost.

On the other hand, when man's mind forgets or through ignorance does not know its part in the One Mind, it soon gets involved in its ideas in the outermost which become crystalized there; and man is thus bound and held by those ideas and it is impossible, to free himself (his consciousness) from them until the light from the One Mind again is able to penetrate through into man's mind, showing him what has befallen him.

Now try to see that everything including man is an avenue of expression of the One Mind,—no, is not an expression of that Mind, for the innermost can only express in the outermost through man's mind. Therefore what seemingly is expressing in the outermost is man's ideas of what are expressing to him from the innermost, but always colored and shaped by man's consciousness of separation from or his identity with the One Mind.

When man's mind is perfectly attuned to the consciousness of the One Mind, the full light or knowing of that Mind can then shine through from the innermost to the outermost, and thereby will man shape his ideas in the outer according to the perfection of the inner that he sees there.

Our chief desire is to have you realize that the One Mind is ever seeking your complete realization of the goodness and perfection of Its ideas, and that especially at this time is pouring Its light with great power into the minds of men, so that all who are in any way attuned to Its consciousness are receiving a rich abundance of Its ideas as never before in the history of the world. Likewise is the sense of separation, the veil that prevents the light of perfect knowing from shining through in its fullness, getting so thin and transparent that many minds are becoming aware of the inner world of the Kingdom, are seeing the beauty, goodness and perfection of everything and everyone there, and are more or less living in Its consciousness.

Can you not feel that Mind everywhere about you, as the Mind that is in you and in everybody, is all-knowing, all-loving and all-powerful; that it therefore knows your every need, loves you with an all-encompassing love, and ever wishes to express in and through you the fullness of Its nature and all the goodness and riches of Its knowing and being?

Think of that Mind as ever pressing from within against your mind seeking to include and unite your consciousness with Its consciousness, so that you not only may receive of the fullness of Its Spiritual blessings, but that you may become a perfect channel of expression so that these blessings can come forth into manifestation in your outer life and affairs.

Remember these blessings are everywhere about you, but are invisible to your human mind only because you think your mind is separate and not a part of the One Mind, where all good and perfect things are eternally present and ever visible. When how could they be separate when that Mind is actually your mind? Ah, dear one, if we could only get you to realize fully this great truth—that that Mind, the only Mind, is indeed your mind, that It knows everything, possesses within itself every desirable thing, always loves you, and always wants you to have the best of everything—to have and be all that It has and is; and that the only thing that is hindering is your mind—its beliefs, its sense of lack and limitation and of being separate!

Seeing this, cannot you then LET GO with your mind —give up that foolish belief, and let the One Mind have Its way entirely with you? To let go is to desire nothing anymore and to resist nothing, to give your consciousness over wholly to It, to care for nothing only that you are no longer hindering Its expression in and through you.

That is all you need do. You must try to do nothing of what It presses you to do or say. It will do this always out of a great love, so that you may know Its will for you.

No more must you rebel against anything, nor refuse whatever is placed before you to do. But instead you must let go, turn within and let the Loving Mind there show you what to do and how to do it.

Ever seek to keep strong hold on those old impulses of your mind that would from habit start to say or do something out of the old sense of self, of lack and limitation and of separation. It is from such impulses that all trouble and inharmony spring. When the mind ever seeks to be united with its Source, to be directed and used by It, can you not see from what is shown above that only goodness, harmony, peace and happiness must result?

When there is only one mind the beauty, goodness and perfection of the within must come into the without, for they are always pressing against man's mind seeking to express through it—their only medium of expression so that the without may be united with the within and the Kingdom of Heaven may actually manifest upon Earth.

Let us sum up the practical application of the above. If it is a matter of healing, remember that as the One Mind - sees and knows you, you (or your patient) are perfect now and always have been. It is your mind that must stop thinking differently; it must also stop forcefully trying to see perfection, and instead you need only to direct the mind's attention within to the One Mind, Life, God—whichever is easier for you, and then let go. This releases your mind from the influence of the impressions from outer physical sensations and their mental pictures, and leaves the One Mind free to reveal and true nature, to come forth and possess your consciousness an express forth and be your True Self, When the mind is perfectly still and is turned within expectant, the channel is open and the One Life can then come forth freely through your consciousness unto perfect manifestation.

You can see that will apply in a similar way to where there is a consciousness of lack or limitation of finances. As all things come from the One Mind and that Mind is in everyone, wherever there is a need -it is felt by that Mind and when your channel is open, unimpeded by fear, doubts or worry, it will surely fulfill that need.

When you know the truth, the truth will make you free when you always act in that truth.

We are approaching another Easter time, the time of Resurrection when the soul is given additional opportunity of freeing itself from the control of the flesh and its sense of separation and of lifting the consciousness of its human mind into oneness with its soul consciousness, where it may actually see and be with the Lord and its soul companions of the Kingdom "in the air."

Let every disciple strive during Lent to put self and its claims. wholly aside, allowing the Christ to rule in every thought, word and act. This means that even the desire to attend the Easter Services in the Spirit must yield to Him: for surely He knows of such desire and wishes and purposes that you shall attend—when self's longings no longer -interfere and permit it. Think this over and try to place yourself altogether in His hands, making your mind an empty channel into which He can pour His Consciousness.

VII. MAN, THE IMAGE AND LIKENESS OF GOD

PAPER #40, April 1932.

In the first chapter of Genesis we are told that God created man in His own image and likeness. Pythagoras tells us that the Universal Creator formed two things in His own image—the universe with its system of suns, moons and stars, called the macrocosm; and man, in whose nature is duplicated the whole universe, called the microcosm. We would add a third, by stating that our planet earth and all planets are formed in the image and likeness of God.

It stands to reason that if both the universe and man are patterned after God s image, then each planet in the universe as well as all men must follow that same pattern. We will go further and repeat what scientific investigation tells us—that each cell in man's body has the appearance of a miniature man. And we know that science now claims that each atom in man's body is solar system know what he wishes to know about the universe. From in miniature, with a positive proton serving as the sun this it can also be seen why there was written over the around which revolve negative electrons as planets.

In this article we will show man's definite relation and likeness to his mother earth, to his father God, and to the universe. Because we can see only the outer appearance of the earth and the universe and cannot actually see God, we will have to tell you of their inner and real nature by analogy or correspondence, reasoning by pure logic, the method used by philosophers and mystics throughout the ages, and on the accepted principle that "As above, so below. As below, so above.'

You who would essay the Spiritual Heights must train yourself so to reason; for the highest function of mind is to reason, even as the highest function of the heart is intuitive understanding, and working together there is nothing that needs to be known that cannot be known.

Spiritual truths cannot be understood by the separate human mind, but by pure reasoning and analogy—by starting with a known truth and by reasoning step by step, supported by analogy, carrying the consciousness up to a realization of the higher or spiritual truth sought the mind may be lifted-up and united temporarily with the Cosmic Mind and from It receive what is needed. Such is the method largely used in the Impersonal teachings and in all teachings where pure truth is revealed. Unless what is stated is accepted both by your reason and your intuition, it is not truth to you.

In the lifting up process, as the reasoning approaches the truth about to be revealed, you will note that some thing seemingly "above" opens, and a ray of spiritual "light" pours through and "illumines" the mind and what could not be "seen" before is thereby clearly perceived. The lower or separate mind then "accepts" the truth, for it is "lifted up" into the consciousness where that truth is; thus what' was separate for the moment becomes united—in the visioning of that particular truth.

From this you can learn what separateness" really is—that it is but ignorance of the truth. When a mind actually knows a truth, it becomes that truth. It does not need ever again to go through any mental process to reach it: it simply is that truth, which is then an integral part of consciousness, as is knowing how to walk and talk.

But do not confuse true knowing with the above temporary lifting of the consciousness by reasoning to a perception of a truth. That truth thus becomes only an intellectual concept in your separate mind, and is not soul-knowing—which cannot be until by using and living that truth it becomes as natural a part of your conscious" ness as is how to walk and talk; which means that it has been built into and now is a part of your sub- or soul" consciousness. That may take years to accomplish, and may not be accomplished in this life-time—with certain great truths.

From the statement made at the beginning of this article that man is made in the image and likeness of God, it can be seen that the way man may know God is by perfectly knowing his self;- and by the same criterion he may gates of ancient temples as an admonition to those seeking therein to learn wisdom, the words, "Man, Know Thy Self."

By a study of some of the mysteries of man's nature, we will uncover some of the truths regarding the nature of the earth, of the universe and of God.

First, we must clearly realize that man, being the image and likeness of God, cannot be what he appears to mortal sight. There must be an invisible side of his nature that is actually Godlike, partaking of all of God's nature, attributes and powers, if he is God's image; it must always have been so, for so he was -created, which the means that he will always be Godlike.

Then it must be man's misunderstanding and wrong beliefs that prevent his seeing and knowing his true nature. This can easily be accounted for either by the ignorance of his teachers or by his being purposely wrongly taught from the beginning. But the time has now come when man must be taught the truth, and be given the opportunity to realize, to assume and to call upon some of the divine qualities and powers of his God nature, so that he may learn to be and act his true self.

With that purpose in view we will study some of the qualities and powers of this invisible side of man's nature; but not invisible, remember, to all men, for it is visible to certain types of minds more highly endowed than the masses those who have developed their soul and spiritual sight; and such can be numbered by the thousands at the present time.

We have shown you that man is not a physical but a spiritual being; that he is in reality consciousness, an actual center of God's or the Universal Consciousness; that his soul, which is the sum total of the consciousness of the trillions of cells of his so-called physical body, is the real man; and that this soul or real man—the invisible image body of God—is the temple or garment of the Holy Spirit, a Son of God, who being consciously in God's Consciousness is the channel or instrument through which God's will manifests on earth.

Now imagine, if you can, the nature of this Son of God, your Highest Self, the Christ Man living in your invisible image body. Think of the vast powers of this expression of God, all resident within the image-body and of course within the so-called physical body, but under perfect control, and undreamed of by the ordinary human mind. Try to realize that this image-body is actually a body of consciousness, the consciousness of the trillions of cell centers comprising your soul consciousness, and that, even as in your physical body, this consciousness expresses through certain force centers outmanifesting in the physical as glands and nerve plexi, and that these force centers account for and control all the functioning of the chief organs of the body.

If you were endowed with clairvoyant sight and could see clearly an evolved man's soul body, it would appear to you as a scintillating galaxy of stars, each one of which is a force center emanating rays of different coloring and beauty, the vital organs being the most beautiful and appearing ag whirling vortices of light of great brilliancy. In fact the body is such a vast network of psychic centers, connected by innumerable currents of energy crossing each other and coming from these brilliant generators of etheric and magnetic forces, that it is said to resemble a solar system of suns, stars, planets and moons, with comets circling in their orbits among them.

What does that suggest to you? Does it not help to account for the multiplicity of forces operating in your own nature, and expressing themselves in so many ways —as impulses, urges, desires and aspirations of the soul; as thoughts, hopes, longings and ambitions of the mind; as loves and hates, enthusiasms and fears, doubts, worries, anger, remorse, envy, jealousy, irritability and bitterness of the emotions; and as appetites, lusts and passions of the flesh? And can you not see that you, within your being, are a universe of unfathomed powers and possibilities, of untested and uncontrolled forces of tremendous potency?

We will not dwell upon the trillions of cell centers of consciousness of your body representing the inhabitants of your universe (what are you in the Solar Universe as a man but a more complex center of consciousness, and who can tell if in reality you are any greater or any different in consciousness from any cell of your body?) ; nor upon the various organs thereof—the brain, lungs, stomach, bowels, liver, kidneys, generative center, arms, hands, legs and feet, representing the different planetary systems of your universe, with their interplay of forces and direct relations one to another, all working together in perfect harmony to express the life and health of your being. Or we might see certain of the vital organs as representing the planetary forces of your Solar System.

Nor will we more than mention the likeness of the organs of your body to the various races, nations, and governments of the earth, all organized and working with more or less harmony in contributing to the well-being of the planet; leaving it you to follow out these comparisons or analogies as far as you can, knowing that the further you go in the study of them, the more remarkable will you find their likeness.

We wish instead in this article to confine ourselves to a consideration of man's inner nature and the -forces that constitute it, being not so concerned about his outer of physical aspect, although of necessity we will point to certain phases of it manifesting as a direct result of the operation of these forces.

Man is a center of the Universal Consciousness, but his consciousness is naturally affected and influenced by its reactions to the thought and emotional forces constantly flowing into it from without. The consciousness of most men is wide open, because they have not trained their minds to choose what they want in it and to refuse entrance to all distasteful, negative and harmful forces. They have not yet learned that it is such that not only bring all inharmonies into their lives, but they either clog up or close entirely the avenues connecting their minds with the Universal Consciousness, which is always waiting to pour into them the riches of Divine Mind.

Man being a center or Universal Consciousness should then always be connected with it, should be a part of it, all that is in it being over available for his use. This is wholly true of the image and likeness man within, and when the outer consciousness is turned within and is unconcerned and undisturbed by what appears or what comes from without, it naturally is always open to and is constantly receiving from within the blessings of Divine Mind; and consequently the outer life is expressing and in fact is patterned after the divine life manifesting within in the Kingdom of Divine Mind.

This means that all the forces coming from within the Universal Consciousness are good, harmonious and beneficent. Then all that is different or contrary to them must come from without—from men's human minds that think themselves separate and apart from the Divine Mind. Such "separate" thinking naturally creates all kinds of seemingly opposing forces, but which in reality are the forces of the Law seeking to press man's consciousness back again into harmony and union with Divine Mind.

Man not realizing this however resists and fights unceasingly against these forces, seeing only evil and malevolence in them, and thereby causing continual inharmony to manifest in his. body and life. He has not yet learned to cease resisting, to let go and turn within, and thereby to connect up his mind once more with the Divine Mind; and thus permit the Law to press his consciousness back into the harmony from which it had strayed, when that which is manifesting may likewise be released and can also come back into harmony.

This should enable you to trace out the causes of the inharmonious forces now operating in your body and outer life. These causes, remember, are resident in your consciousness, and your consciousness consists of the consciousness of every cell of your body, and likewise of your entire mental atmosphere. Not until you remove the causes and thus cleanse the consciousness of body and thought-life, can harmony manifest. We hope that is now plain.

Realizing now that all is consciousness and that all things that appear exist only as thought pictures in your separate" mind, we will relate your mind and its consciousness first with your so called physical body.

Remember that all being consciousness, then all things take place and all forces operate only in consciousness. Then within your mind we must look for the causes and for the actual forces and things now manifesting in your body and life.

For instance, you think you have a body, but if you will analyze the thought picture in your mind of that body, you will find it traces back to your idea of being a "self" and separate from other selves; when in reality you have no actual body and you are not separate, for you are a Spiritual being, a . center of consciousness in Divine Mind. Just as all the ideas in your consciousness are centers of, within, and a part of your mind, so are you an idea, a center of consciousness of Divine Mind.

So that idea of a self, born after your departure and descent from Eden, eventually developed into a. fully organized mind and in the mind of the race- as a seemingly substantial, physical body. But it was only a thought body that . confined within itself your idea of what you call your "self" when - that idea is pure spirit or consciousness. Try to see this clearly, for it will then enable you to grasp easily what follows.

You have a head, and a face with distinctive features, because of your idea of your mind being housed within the head in a peculiar substance called a brain; and because in your mind are confined all the different attributes and qualities of your soul or consciousness, these qualities outpicture themselves in your face and human personality. In your consciousness you perceived various facts or truths, and in the course of many ages and getting far away from your Edenic consciousness, there appeared in your ' 'head" eyes, through which -as your sight grew dimmer you sought to "see" the spiritual truths that formerly were-so clearly visible- to you. Likewise there appeared ears in your efforts to hear what before easily came to you through intuition. Your weakening faculty of "sensing" the truth developed a nose, and the dulling of your discriminative faculty developed the physical sense of taste.

And now we come to the mouth with its teeth and tongue. What is it for but the ' 'biting off" of a new idea that comes to your attention, "tasting" it carefully to see if you are interested, then "chewing" it finely (meditating upon it, getting out all of its meaning, so that it may be fully understood) extracting all of its juices, and finally "swallowing" it (accepting or believing it as a fact)? Then according to whether or not you have exercised proper discrimination or taste, have thoroughly meditated upon or chewed it, will your stomach (your sub-consciousness) be able perfectly to digest it, build it into blood (life force) and then into your system (your soul consciousness) fully assimilated, thereby creating perfect health (harmony and happiness of mind) .

In like manner -were every organ, feature and part of your body developed, in the effort of different faculties and qualities of the mind and soul to express themselves through this physical shell that covered them. Lungs, heart, liver, kidneys, spleen, sexual organs, bowels, rectum, legs, arms, bones, nerves, hair, all relate to certain forces or activities of the consciousness; and in order fully to know yourself, a study of this relation will prove highly profitable.

It is not within the province of this and future articles to indicate all the connections between the body -and consciousness, leaving it to those who feel led to such study to trace them out for themselves. Those who wish help in this direction can find it in a remarkable book by F. L. Rawson, entitled "Life Understood;" published in England, which we can procure on order. It. contains highly illuminative instruction on the law of right thinking and is used as a text-book by thousands of metaphysicians and students of the Rawson and "Absolute" schools of thought all over the world. It contains 700 pages and its price is $5.25 postpaid.

Because of lack of room in this issue we will continue this subject in the next Paper, aiming to round it out more fully and then to extend the relation and comparison of man's consciousness to that of the Earth and our Solar System. Thus showing how man is actually God, and how God is truly expressing Himself identically in the Solar System, in the earth, and in man; but 'in each only as much of Himself as the consciousness of each is unfolded enough to accept and permit; yet all the time all of the consciousness they being His consciousness.

A VISION OF THE NEW DAY

Many have reported visions telling of the doom awaiting the Old Order and its institutions, but we have had none sent us that contain so definite a promise of what will follow the passing of the Old Order as the one described in the letter below:

"Dear Ones:

I have just come out of an hour's glorious meditation, during which I seemed to become as a white dove, taking my part in a most beautiful Vision, which I must send to you before I take up the day's duties.

"From before a dark cave in what seemed to be a rugged mountain, a huge stone began to roll forward. As it moved there appeared tongues of fire which went before it, -while out of the blackness behind it there came the Christ. In His right hand He held a shining sword, on the blade were the words "Truth" and "Love," one on each side, which seemed to be written in what appeared to be scintillating diamonds, that flashed as He turned it. On His left arm there sat what seemed a white dove, holding in its beak a leaf.

' 'As the Christ moved forward, the stone and the fire moved on before Him and behind Him there came, almost as if it streamed out from Him, a brilliant light, which was fan-shaped and seemed to reach all over the world, as did the tongues of fire. As the Christ moved onward, the stone became less and less, also the fire, but in its passing over the world it had wiped out all negation. All around white doves flew, dropping leaves onto the world.

"After the stone and the fire had passed, I saw that the guns of war had become harvesting machines, and the men who had been crouched behind machine-guns were milking cows; instead of the rumble and roar of war, there was only the hum of industry, the singing of happy contented hearts, and the joyous noise of little children at play. And it seemed that all "heads" of governments were no more, but Christ was the Head; and that He had appointed one over each state or country to guide and counsel. All was peace, plenty, love and unity of Brotherhood. A great peace fills my heart

This vision, because of its true symbolism, makes the interpretation we give more convincing in its prophecy and more happily encouraging to those who have been inclined to look only on the dark and destructive side of the change now taking place in the world preparatory to the coming of the New Order, It is truly a promise of what will be, and we are glad to pass it on to our dear ones. This friend has not yet had Papers 37 and 38 and so was not influenced in her meditation by what they contain.

The dark cave in the rugged mountain from before which a huge stone began to roll downward, symbolizes the cave or hollowness in the mountain of materiality, in which are confined the dark forces of selfishness and greed and their progeny that always breed destruction and disintegration, but which eventually loosen the great stone of self as its rapacity grows so that it destroys everything in its path as it rolls down the mountain side to the valley below, where such forces do not thrive. The tongues of fire were these forces accompanying the stone and aiding in completing the destruction, so that nothing remained of anything that formerly appeared on the mountain side.

All unaware of His Presence, the Christ, - the master and ruler of all forces, when they become too powerful, releases them from control and they immediately begin to destroy their own creations and all that have been built on that mountain. But He, the great Spirit of Light and Love, always follows close after, flashing His sword of Truth and sending forth

His messages of comfort carried by doves of peace to all able to receive them; while the Light from His Army of the Heavenly Host illumines the consciousness of those hearts and minds that are turned to Him, enabling them to see and escape the destruction that overtakes others.

After He has allowed the stone of selfishness and the fires of greed to destroy and burn up all that could be consumed, there was left a clean world in which such dark forces could no longer thrive, for in it only Light and Love ruled, the hearts of men, and the darkness of self could not approach, no more than can darkness be where there is a brilliant light.

In this vision we are shown what will naturally follow in such a world. It is a beautiful confirmation, dear ones, of! the Master's promise explained in the last two Papers, and as reported in Mat. 24 and 25, and assures us that the time is soon here when "That Day" will be realized. May we all watch carefully and pray that as many be saved as possible.

EASTER

We are sorry that not all will receive this Paper before Easter, but conditions were such that it could not be gotten out earlier.

This has been a remarkable Winter in more ways than one. It has been different—the fore part being more like November and the real Winter here in the East not appearing until March.

But many of you know that even as has the weather seemed, so have the internal forces of your own nature cumulated so that it has almost been a crucifixion through which you have been passing the last month. In one way or another have you been tried almost to the breaking-point.

Can you not see that it is but the effort of the Christ Force within your nature and within all nature trying to throw off all bonds that are holding It back, and attempting to burst through and take possession and express the fullness and perfection of the Christ Life? The harder your trials have been, the surer have there been burned away qualities and tendencies that have hindred the expression of your Spiritual nature. It is His nature preparing His body for the Resurrection. No, not His physical body, but His image and likeness body, His Christ body within all nature, so that it will be ready for Easter morn.

Will you not then cease resisting—and compel your human mind, which alone resists, to let go utterlv and permit this Christ Force, His Consciousness, the Universal

Life urge within you, to come forth and take possession and do Its will, live Its life in you, without hindrance of any kind. Oh, if we could only get you to do this—then you will truly know what is the resurrection body, and what is the real meaning of Easter.

Listen to this that came while we were writing this article :

"I recently had an experience. I woke up one morning about 6 A. M. I dressed and went down stairs. Had had trouble sleeping because of a cough. As I sat by the fireside smoking, my first thought was, what a nuisance a cough is to disturb one's sleep, Following arose the thought of the physical body being a handicap. How it hurts when it falls down, gets too hot or too cold, gets tired or sick, etc. Then I thought, 'Why, I am Divine—I am a Spiritual Being! This thought was so strong that it made me feel I am Divine—and I had the consciousness of my true existence as Divine Consciousness. Also -that the sensation or consciousness of my physical body was a falsity, a lie.

"While I remained aware of my physical body, yet at the same time I was experiencing that only the I AM plus consciousness, was truth. I kept feeling that my body is a lie, an untruth. All things affecting my body also are lies. I thought, how strange! I am body conscious, yet this perception of a body is false. I also thought, all things that ever happened are lies. Only the I AM is true, and it is perfect and dwells on a high plane of consciousness where all is perfection, goodness, peace, love, ease—an Utopia.

"Also it occurred to me that all this depression, kidnappings, hunger, want, poverty in the world is a lie, a non-reality, a delusion put into the world mind; and the real, the true and the beautiful seldom enters or is perceived by man's mind.

"Also I thought, whatever happens to me, to my physical consciousness, is not true. The real I of me is the Infinite and cannot be affected by the finite. All that does not concern the real Me is but appearance, is an illusion of the senses. And the world of appearance, what our five senses report, although seemingly real, yet it never approaches the reality of the True World of the I AM. "To once isolate one's self in consciousness with this Real I, to hold in that consciousness for awhile; to fix the process or faculty of being '1 AM" conscious—is to dwell in the awareness of one's Godhood, and to become conscious of one's Wisdom and Power.

"I however realize that in my experiences, what is revealed to me does me or any one else no good unless I can use this Power and Wisdom. To the man who is poverty-stricken, sick, etc., how futile to tell him these appearances of limitations are but delusions. So I have always sought to be conscious of the power to create and to correct untruths in consciousness and appearances instantly.

"In some experiences of the past I sat imagining myself as healing different ones, raising dead people; gazing out of the window and realizing all that I had to do was to speak, and the flat plains would rise to mountain heighths; also to gaze at the fields in Winter, to speak, and have the snow dissolve and the farms produce according to my desire and will."

Think on the above until you get all of its true meaning, and you will get a glimpse of what is your Resurrection Body, and how to rise into and work in -it. For that body is only that of your Christ Consciousness, where you see not with mortal eyes, but with God's -eyes and understanding His image and likeness in all men—His perfection; likewise see the

goodness and perfection in all things and all conditions—their eternal harmony; for is not He all in all?

And knowing this will not your Word of Truth drive out all error in consciousness and destroy the manifest lie?

Try it and see! The Word of Truth spoken from a consciousness that KNOWS is all powerful.

VIII. AS ABOVE, SO BELOW"

PAPER No. 41 MAY, 1932

We know there are many that are deeply interested in our study of man's nature and our showing its relation to universal nature—to that of the cell, the planet and the universe. So we will continue that study herein, knowing that we will reach both heights and depths of consciousness that may bring illumination to some and will surely repay the efforts of all who follow with us.

In the April Paper were shown the relation of the organs of seeing, hearing, smelling, tasting, chewing, swallowing, digesting and assimilating, to certain spiritual faculties or capacities of the mind. These in their efforts to express and maintain themselves in the lower vibrations aroused by the mind's idea of being a self and separate in consciousness from other centers of mind, gave but short-lived satisfaction to the soul, soon weakening these higher faculties' powers of functioning; and through the mind's continued belief in such separation, in the course of time there came into expression the complex organism now known as the physical body.

Thinking you may be interested in learning more about the connection between man's mental and physical functioning, before passing on to the main theme of this article we will suggest other relations for you to consider and contemplate at your leisure.

The head, for instance, represents the capacity of the mind with all its different faculties to receive and utilize the ideas coming from other centers of Divine Mind. It is the Wisdom center; it tops, rules and directs all other capacities and represents the mind of Christ. Christ is the head of the body of Divine Truth, the perfect mind of the perfect body—the image and likeness body, of which you have learned.

The lungs represent mind's capacity to receive (inhale) the Breath of God (His Love—actually His life) to utilize His Love by supplying it (as His Life or vitality) to that faculty (the heart) which distributes It to all other faculties of mind for Christ's use and then gives back to God (exhales) that Love, with mind's reaction or response to It, for God's further use.

The heart represents the capacity of mind to receive the Love-life of God and to distribute it to all the other faculties of mind, thus connecting and uniting them in the One Life and One Consciousness, so that they will co-operate and function in the perfect harmony of God's Love-life. The heart is the Love center, the connecting faculty of mind that links the innermost of consciousness with the outermost. It is that center which is the Way, the Truth and the Life; no man cometh unto the Father but through it, and nothing cometh from the Father except through it.

The arms represent the power of mind to utilize and pass on to other centers of consciousness (other men) the ideas that are received from God's Mind.

The legs represent mind's power of spiritually supporting and sustaining all of God's Truth and Love, and of carrying them swiftly and easily from one center of consciousness to another (from one man to another, or from one idea to another) .

The skin represents mind's belief in God's Love ever surrounding and protecting each center of consciousness in His body of Truth.

The hairs represent the lines of force over which God's Love-life flows and enters the mind, thus keeping alive the power of His Love.

The bones represent the structure of Truth which supports and around which is built the whole body of God's Ideas or of Truth in mind.

These are but a few OF the many organs and parts of the body which are the outpicturing of faculties, powers and capacities of mind in action—enough to help you to relate others, if you are interested in discovering such relation. But remember, they are pictures that exist only in the "separate" mind; for in your Christ Consciousness you would "see" them for what they are—activities of Divine Mind operating in and through you, one of Its centers,—you, the microcosm of the macrocosm.

As all is consciousness, which this helps you clearly to see, then all activities of consciousness are forces that operate either in the human mind and outmanifest in the human body, or in the earth mind and outmanifest in the earth body. And we can add also—in the universal mind and outmanifest in the body of the universe.

Man has plenty of evidences of the operation of these mental forces in his body, in the many inharmonies and diseases he has to suffer as a result of his not harmonizing his thinking with God's Love and Truth, which God is ever seeking to express in and through man's mind. But man, believing his mind separate fr.om God's Mind, has, as it were, through such belief, shut the door upon God, so that His Love cannot reach him; he cannot feel its healing, vitalizing, strengthening and renewing power. So counter forces are set and the opposite of Love and Truth manifests—selfishness, greed, envy, jealousy and lust for power; generating their brood of fears, worries, doubts, anxieties and discouragement; engendering lies deceit, hatred, treacheries, sins and crimes; all of which are causing the inharmonies and diseases so common in mankind everywhere.

But think you these counter forces stop in man? No they go forth from him as a center and naturally affect every other center of mind in any way attuned to man; which includes his fellowmen, influencing them and engendering in them similar forces. And these forces, in their interplay between these human centers, naturally affect the earth mind, or the mental atmosphere surrounding the earth, including the consciousness of what is called nature—the elemental forces of earth, water, fire and air; in a similar way to how each man's thought atmosphere affects his personal life and affairs and those of everyone who comes near him.

Now what is the earth? Have you ever thought just what it is or what it represents?

You say the earth is a planet? On a clear, cloudless night have you ever wondered what are all those mil lion, billion or trillion points of light you see in the heavens—what they "represent?'

What if we should say that you as a soul are a light in the great firmament of heaven (remember, that firmament is also but the attempt of man´s mind to see and picturize its concept of the vast height and extent of the Divine or Heavenly Consciousness) —perhaps at present you are a very dim light and imperceptible at a distance? But as your soul is able more and more to reflect and give out the light ever -shining deep within it, that light will grow brighter and brighter and in the ages to come you may win a place in a constellation that will be known to a future humanity.

For remember you as a soul in the far distant ages will win to the exalted state of a Son of God, even to such a Son of God as is now your Father in Heaven, your Higher Self. Do not get confused by this statement, but recall that your Higher self climbed to His high estate as a Son of God through countless ages before this earth was, and His light is now a brilliant star shining, in one of the constellations connected with our Solar System.- While He descended in consciousness from His Celestial estate in order to redeem your soul,   which comprises the sum total of His mistakes committed in consciousness in a previous world period, His Spirit still shines in the heavens, and from It you derive all that you are. But you as a soul, with His help in the ages to come, will climb into oneness of consciousness with the Ruler of the planet Earth, and then with the Ruler of our Solar System, whom we know - as our Father-God; even as your Higher Self long eons ago attained oneness of consciousness with that of the Ruler of the planet which give Him birth, and then eons later with the God of our Solar System; which earned for Him His title as a Son of God.

From this you may have glimpsed, remembering that what appears outwardly in form always embodies an idea or a center of consciousness, that the earth is not actually a mere physical planet, but like all the other planets is a center of Consciousness of Divine Mind—shall we say, is one of the vital centers of the Body of our Father-God, the Ruler of our Solar System, representing one of the higher faculties of His Mind; even as the head, lungs, heart, liver, kidneys, spleen, and generative organs are vital centers of our bodies and represent the higher faculties and capacities of our minds.

In other words, the earth is the outer representation of the great Spiritual Being Who must be the Ruler of the planet earth; the One Who is responsible for the- life expression of all consciousness on- the planet—from that of the mineral kingdom to that of humanity. You often hear the term "Mother Earth." What then is more natural than that this

Being is the one who ' 'generates": the life forces of the planet, who "steps down" the Solar- force from the Father-God's Mind, reconditions it and makes it adaptable and available for our use and for all dependent upon Her for their life? We call this Being -"Her," but in reality She as a Divine Being is both male and female, even as is our Father-God. She gives birth to, feeds and nourishes all life from Her bosom, but only that life which our Father-God, Himself, first fecundated in Her and fructified.

" Therefore, this Ruler of the Earth must be one of the "Sons of God," even as are our Higher Selves—only of a much higher degree than they; and from all that has been written about and claimed for Him it may well be assumed that the Ego or Soul whom we know as Jesus, the Christ, is that Ruler. At least, it would seem that He is the present Ruler, although many claim Jehovah is the God or Ruler of the Earth. The Hebrew Scriptures declare this. Jesus spoke not of Jehovah, but always of -His Father-God Who sent Him. He openly states His One ness with the Father—that those who have seen Him have seen the Father. That could mean only one of two things —that He actually was the Father in manifestation, superceding Jehovah-God of the old testament; or that He, Himself was Jehovah, the representative of His Father, the Solar God. There are those who claim the latter.

But to us it is immaterial. The point we wish particularly to make is that the Earth is actually a Spiritual or Divine Being in Whose consciousness we live, move and have our being. For we certainly derive our life, all our power to move, act and be, from the food we eat and the air we breathe, both of which must consist of the sub' stance and vitality of the Earth nature—the nature of the Being Who is expressing Himself outwardly as the planet Earth, and Who is serving as our terrestrial Mother. But remember, we have stated that She receives all of Her life and power from the Sun, our Solar God, -Her Father-in-Heaven, Who enables Her to do and be all that She does and is.

We now ask you to think of this Being as a Man in the image and likeness of God, even as are all men in their true nature; and that the earth with all on it is only His outer physical garment, just as our physical bodies are our outer garments. Then we can say that each human being is but a cell in the body of humanity, that body representing the human or mental part of His nature; while animals represent the lower or emotional part, vegetation the vital or life-giving part, and minerals merely the structural or supporting part.

Think on this until you get its full meaning, and then try to realize that what humanity is now thinking and feeling, and the forces thereby generated, are affecting the force centers of the psychic body of our Mother Earth; for does she not have a mental, psychic, vital and physical body, the same as we? And if humanity has not harmonized its thinking with God's Truth and Love, and instead has set up the counter forces of selfishness, greed, envy, jealousy and lust for power, engendering all of the consequent negative and destructive forces aforementioned— who can deny that such forces are not rampant in the world today—can you not see what terrible diseases must now be manifesting within the body of our terrestrial Mother?

How long is: Her body going to stand it? Those conversant with the true conditions existing, know that She cannot endure it much longer. Nature will stand just so much, whether it be in a man or in a god; then -it. rebels, and with a mighty effort it throws off all restraining influences, purges the poison from the system, and brings it back once more into perfect health and harmony.

We urge that all read again the 16th. chapter of "The Impersonal Life," on "The Christ and Love," especially the parts on pages 133 and 134, where the full meaning and application of the foregoing is shown. You can easily see that what is stated in this chapter is the actual condition of humanity today.

We hardly need to point out that all seismic disturbances are evidences of Nature's reaction to the inharmonious thoughts and emotional turmoil engendered by man's selfishness and greed, and resulting in the present badly diseased condition of humanity. What are thunderstorms but the conflict of the forces of love and hate in the earth's mental atmosphere brought to a climax, drawing down from the Heavenly Mind flashes of Truth that illumine men's minds and soon clear the mental atmosphere of antagonism and misunderstanding?. What are storms at sea but the destructive waves of emotion that at times almost overwhelm mind and soul? What are earthquakes but the quaking of the soul in its fear and terror at the disease gnawing at its vitals, and at yielding and succumbing to its dire effects? And what are volcanic eruptions but the efforts of the soul to rid mind and heart of all the poisonous thoughts and feelings that make impossible its longed for union with Divine Mind and for happiness, harmony and peace that awaits?

Can you not now see that what is happening to humanity, both in the conditions manifesting in its outer life— poverty, hardship, suffering, and may be later famine, pestilence, war—and in the continually increasing catastrophes resulting from seismic activities, is caused by man's thoughtless, senseless and foolishly destructive thinking, speech and action, ever pushed into such expression by that malignant disease eating its way through his vital organs?

What is that disease? Entitized selfishness and greed, which will gradually gather unto itself the life and sub" stance of the bulk of humanity—if not soon halted by Nature, the Ruler of the Planet, God—the Three-in-One.

Think you man can stop it? No, it has now gone too far for that. Only God and His Army of Light can prevail against this arch-enemy of God and humanity, who is ever playing on man's ignorance, using his dastardly sophistries to subvert and destroy the good in men's minds. And God will not act until humanity has sufficiently learned its lessons, and has evidenced it by enough of mankind turning to Him in humble and sincere repentance, asking to be saved. He is but waiting for that time.

In the meantime, let us consider what is happening to the Divine Being whom we have called the Ruler of our planet Earth. If humanity is suffering, and humanity represents His mentality, can you not see how He must also be suffering? And if this disease is as terrible as it has been pictured, and it is caused entirely by the wrong and evil thinking of humanity, the results of which He has to bear, can you not understand that He must be going through a crucifixion similar in degree to what Jesus underwent on the cross?

For is not this Great One being crucified on the cross of matter, the cross of man's material desires, and does not His Spirit know, even as Jesus knew, that only by giving His Body thus to be used (which means His mentality, for all things take place only in consciousness, remember) can all that which makes up His Consciousness, the consciousness of every cell of His body of humanity, be cleansed and purified, so that it can become a perfect channel for the expression and use of the One Mind?

There is a wonderful truth in all this, dear friends, proving that all is really One, nothing is separate or living unto itself alone. For what one man suffers, every man, every cell, every atom in the body of humanity must suffer. And therefore must the earth, must Christ, must God also suffer. Man is but a cell in the earth's body, an atom in God's Body. And when any single atom in God's Body is out of harmony, the whole universe feels and knows it, and reacts to bring it back into harmony. That is the Law of Life, of Love, of Harmony.

Remember what has been taught, however; that it is only seeming inharmony; for in God's Mind there cannot be inharmony—He being all-wise, all-loving, all-powerful; and what seems to be inharmony is but the disturbance caused by the switching or counterbalancing of forces, as they press the disturbing factors in consciousness and in outer conditions of cell, man, nation and planet back again into their true state.

But all this seeming inharmony will soon come to an end. The pressure of the Law is becoming so strong that in the—near-future the Great Being now suffering on the cross will say, "It is finished," and the earth and its humanity will come into their own.

For in very truth, He who is the life of humanity is now being crucified; for is He not also the soul of humanity. Many have the cries gone up, "My God, My God, why hast thou forsaken me!" Which is the cry of the soul when it has reached the extreme of endurance.

But after the crucifixion comes the resurrection always will it follow. For Jesus' persecution and death on the cross, and final resurrection and ascension, was a universal symbol of what will and must happen, not only to individual man, but to each nation, race, planet and universe not to speak of each cell and atom that compose them.

Therefore, take heart, dear ones, and know that what we are now enduring must be gone through with—if we would prepare and be ready for the glorious resurrection that will surely follow. Think only of what awaits.

Now that you know, even as Jesus and the Blessed One Who is our terrestrial Mother knew, can you not go forward as did They, in the realization that by our sacrifice does the whole world move forward toward its final redemption?

VISIONS AND DREAMS

Many are seeing visions these days and having dreams which they feel are of deep significance. Many have written relating to us their dreams and visions, and we have tried to give them such interpretations as we could. But not always were we able to give them full explanations,

because so much left untold, little but important details, impressions felt at the time, and conditions leading up to and which usually brought on the dream or vision, as a response of the soul or the Higher Self in its effort to help solve the problem or difficulty the human mind was facing.

In this article we will try to enable you to interpret your own dreams and visions; for you must realize that they come to you for a purpose, and if you make no determined effort to get their meaning, their coming is of no value or use; for every one was intended to help you in the very difficulty that at the time was disturbing your peace of mind.

First know that all such dreams and visions are either actual experiences of your soul (always the case in dreams), or the veil is temporarily lifted between the physical and the inner world (in visions) and you are permitted to see or hear what is transpiring in the soul realm.

Now if you can realize that all things come first into expression in the soul realm and later outmanifest in the physical, you can see the importance of understanding what is taking place in the inner realm and of trying to grasp the meaning of the symbolic outpicturing you are permitted to see there.

For in spirit, as it is called because of being different from and opposite to matter, you enter a fourth dimension of consciousness, where it is impossible to convey to the human mind (which knows of life and things only in terms of form, or of three dimensions—length, breadth and thickness) facts and conditions that have no translatable terms in which to describe them. Therefore, through a peculiar process which we will later explain, ideas and thoughts are illustrated to the human mind in the form of pictures, and it is these pictures alone that are brought back to normal consciousness.

If you will study your mind when a new idea or thought comes to you, you will note that immediately a picture forms in your consciousness, illustrating that idea. And it is usually that picture that is impressed on the memory and enables you to recall the idea when needed. In exactly the same way does memory serve you when you recall a dream or vision. For in the higher realms of the fourth dimension—where awakened souls live, language and speech are not used; one soul communes with another entirely by means of thought. But every thought automatically forms for itself a picture or thought form in consciousness, and so it is these thought forms, illustrations of the incidents and experiences through which you passed, that you see and remember when coming back into full physical consciousness.

Understanding this, you can see the necessity of not being unduly interested in the pictures or combination of thought forms, no matter how beautiful or wonderful they are, but of going back and studying each detail of the pictures in an effort to recall the ideas and thoughts that gave them birth. This you must do, if you would get the real meaning and purpose for you of the dreams and visions.

In other words, by focusing your mind upon any detail of the dream or vision, you find you are drawn back into the consciousness you were in when the thought picture of it was formed; -and thereby you will see, or rather know, just what were the ideas or thoughts flowing into your mind at the time regarding the events then transpiring. You will know this by these same ideas flooding into your mind again, for you will have connected up with their vibrations, which are never lost and can be contacted at will at any time by one who knows and wishes to do so. All you have to do is to watch carefully the impressions that come and note that they open up to your mind surprising inner meanings of the pictures that before were unperceived.

This is exactly what we do when trying to interpret them for you; we concentrate upon the picture that forms in our mind from your description, and then note the impressions that flow in as we are able more or less to enter the consciousness you were in while going through the experience. You having the complete picture in your mind, and knowing all the details, should be far better able to get a perfect interpretation of it than are we.

Try to prove this. All it requires is concentration upon the dream or vision while trying to recall it in detail, and the ability to note the impressions that flow into your mind while doing so. If you do this faithfully, you cannot help but get results.

THE EASTER CEREMONIES

This year we have purposely not spoken of the Easter Ceremonies and are not giving any description of them as in former years; because we wanted you instead to get the Inner meaning of Easter, its spiritual and cosmic significance, what the crucifixion and resurrection taking place in nature really mean. In the first article of this Paper we tried to show that.

Too many of our friends, we found, were more concerned about being able consciously to attend the ceremonies than they were about learning their true significance, and thereby earning the right to be in attendance. By that we mean, they were seeking more the power and honor of being there than they were the spiritual growth which alone gives them the right. Not consciously was this so to them, for they thought they were doing everything they could to prepare themselves. But is it not true there was a strong desire to be present—because of the wonder and glory of participating in such an experience?

Can you not see that this desire is of the personality, and because of its nature more than anything else it prevented your rising in consciousness to that of the soul which would permit of your being where it was?

Spiritual growth, and particularly such special gift of unfoldment, for it seems it is a gift and is bestowed by the Master by His Grace, do not come as a result of effort—only by living the life—His life, by giving one's self and all one's desires over wholly to Him.

The very thing that is dearest to our hearts and is so strongly desired—even if it is spiritual growth itself, may therefore be the one thing that is holding back our growth and preventing the consummation of what is so dear to us.

Remember, nothing that savors of the self can be taken with us into the Kingdom; all of its qualities, its likes and dislikes, its desires, hopes and aspirations, must be left behind. Our human minds and personalities must be pure and desireless, instruments become selfless and perfect for the Master's use. This is hard for many to accept and understand, but study it over until you do understand.

We have tried to show you something in the above, and it has relation to what was said in the preceding article about visions and dreams. For if you can understand it, the Easter ceremonies were in the nature of both a dream and a vision. In fact, your human mind could conceive of the true and wonderful spiritual experience of the Cosmic Ceremonies celebrated all through the Easter period only as we pictured them to you in previous years, or as you would experience them in a dream or vision, no matter how conscious you were or how natural it would seem to be to you.

Therefore be content to wait until by natural growth the Spirit within you awakens the faculties that will enable you both to see and comprehend the spiritual meaning of the Cosmic events - of which you will then be an actual participator, because of being a conscious and an integral factor in their expression.

IX. THE SEVEN SPIRITS BEFORE THE THRONE"

PAPER No. 42 JUNE, 1932

In the last two Papers, using the law of analogy. "As above, so below," and "As below, so above," we showed you from the standpoint of consciousness, the consciousness of your Spiritual Self, how everything that appears to your mortal mind is but an idea or center of consciousness, a center of force, an expression of the One Mind. We also showed that it is only the "separate" human mind, in its attempt to understand and interpret such ideas pressing from within, that builds in its consciousness forms, organs and organisms to house and confine the forces of these ideas, not knowing that such forms, organs and organisms exist only in its consciousness as mental pictures and have no actual reality except as symbols of the ideas they hide.

You have seen how the mind has outpictured to itself certain centers of its own consciousness—faculties and qualities of the soul, as different organs and parts making up the physical body in its efforts to express the life force pushing forth from within. You have also seen how it has pictured the great centers of cosmic forces expressing through what is called the "planet" earth. And now we will conclude this series of explanations of the relationships of things that appear to the spiritual realities expressing through them, by considering for awhile what is our Solar System and the different cosmic forces that comprise it.

We will of course start with the Sun. From what we have said about the Earth and the Divine Being manifesting as the physical planet that is our terrestrial home, you can see now that the Sun must be but the symbol of the wondrous Being who is the Father God and Ruler of all things appearing to dwell within the confines of our world system. That would mean that the seven planets now admitted as belonging to our Solar System —-Mercury, Venus, Earth, Mars, Jupiter, Saturn and Uranus, named in the order of their supposed proximity to the Sun, Mercury being the nearest to it and Uranus the fartherest away, and all said to be "revolving" around the Sun would also be Divine Beings, having some very mystical relation to the Father God and to each other.

We will consider the Sun and the Solar System first as the "Grand Man," in Whom the whole system and all in it live, move and have their being. For you must remember that as all is consciousness, it is in God's— this Great Being's Consciousness that all exist, each individual thing from atom to planet being an idea or center of His Consciousness.

As the so-called planets are the greatest and therefore the chief centers of that Consciousness, they must be similar to the chief centers of man's consciousness—the brain or thinking center, the heart or emotional center, the solar plexus or life center, and the generative organs or creative center, including the three higher functional centers of the mind, which we will indicate later.

We might say that Mercury represents the thinking faculty of God's Consciousness; Venus the emotional quality; Earth the life center; Mars the creative faculty; Jupiter, the religious or devotional quality; Saturn, the testing, restraining, disciplining, -purifying, perfecting qualities; and Uranus, the uniting, freeing, all-seeing and all-knowing faculties. For as God includes within Himself all faculties, qualities and powers, as well as all life, so must these work through forces or agencies of His own nature; and as the whole Solar System is but the expression of His Nature. or Being, then all the forces operating in our Solar System must be under the direction of those great faculties of His Consciousness, represented outwardly as the seven planets mentioned, but now known inwardly to be Divine Beings and Who are actually the "Seven Spirits before the Throne of God."

Just as all earth men are centers of God's consciousness, even if no more than atoms in His cosmic body, so we could say that these Seven Great Spirits are the seven divine faculties or qualities of His God-Mind, but manifesting as the great radiations of Light, Life and Force known as the seven planets of our Solar System. And even as the seven centers of our physical bodies, representing the seven greater faculties and qualities of our minds, are each composed of billions of cell centers of consciousness, so would all living things on these seven planets be but cells or atoms, minute centers of consciousness, of the Great Beings Who are ensouling them.

There is much more that could be said of the Sun and the planetary bodies of these Great Beings, all of Whose forces, life and nature are comprising and expressing the life and consciousness of the Great One we know as God. But we will leave it to you to receive direct from Him within you what He wishes you to know, after suggesting one or two more lines of approach.

Even as He symbolizes Himself to you as the Sun, the source of all light, heat and power, as well as of all life and consciousness on our planet Earth and on all other planets "revolving around" the Sun, you can now see that He is in reality not without and afar off up in the skies, but is that Center deep within you, that is radiating Himself out to the circumference of your human mind, and thereby forming with your consciousness a mighty world of forces, powers and activities comparable only to what you can imagine are all about you in the outer world extending to the farthermost reaches of our visible Solar System.

Yes, all of the forces, powers and activities that you can thus imagine, are actually within you, for there is nothing that is outside your consciousness. Therefore all the wisdom, power and possibilities of every being in the Solar System, which includes that of the Great Beings Who are the Rulers of the seven planets, and that of very God, Himself, are within you, are a part of you, ready to respond to and serve you in your need, whenever you call upon them fully knowing this truth. Think of this until you grasp its mighty significance.

Then here is something new, never before given out, but which in the light of what has been shown above you can now see for yourself must be true.

The Solar Universe is pictured to you with the Sun as a center and with the planets Mercury, Venus, Earth, Mars, Jupiter, Saturn and Uranus revolving around it.

But we say that instead of these being planets revolving around the Sun, they are realms of consciousness surrounding the central consciousness that is called the Sun; the first realm being the consciousness called Mercury, or the mental world; the second realm called Venus, or the emotional world; the third realm being the Earth, or the desire world, in which the bulk of its humanity is now manifesting; the fourth realm being Mars, or the world of creative forces, through which earth humanity has evolved; while the fifth, sixth, and seventh realms of Jupiter, Saturn and Uranus are the Divine worlds through which the Sons of God, the Higher Selves of humanity, descended or involved Themselves, and from which They worked while evolving the consciousness of Their former miscreations up through the mineral, vegetable and animal kingdoms to the stage where They could ensoul it. This was finally accomplished in the Mars realm, with the help of the Great Being Who was its Ruler, and of His lieutenants; and the further unfoldment of consciousness in individual souls then proceeded under the immediate direction of the Sons of God in that realm known as the Earth state of consciousness, residing between the Mars and Venus realms.

In other words, the consciousness of what we call the Earth humanity is now in that state of redemption where (having passed through the realm of Mars, called the generative or creative realm, where all forms from the lowest and densest of the mineral kingdom to those of domestic animals, the highest of the animal kingdom, were created" for the use of man) having evolved up through the lower stages of the desire world, it has reached the higher desire planes of consciousness. Which accounts for man's being constantly torn between the desires of his higher and lower nature, although many souls have gone beyond and are now feeling the call of the lower Venus or love forces within; while a lesser number have reached the higher planes of Venus, a few having entered the Mercury planes of consciousness, and some even the higher planes.

Now while Venus or the emotional realm, and Mercury, the mental realm, are the two remaining realms through which the human consciousness must pass before entering the Sun realm, we must remember that in the Father's House or Consciousness there are many mansions or realms; and in reality the Jupiter, Saturn and Uranus realms which seem to be beyond or outside the Mars realm, are actually the three higher, Spiritual, Celestial and Divine realms through which humanity's consciousness must pass before reaching the center of the Sun—the Father's Throne. They are the three realms, as was shown, through which the Sons of God descended or involved in order to reach and redeem the earth consciousness. They necessarily have to return through these realms, but will bring with Them the consciousness or the souls They have redeemed. It is because of these three planets or realms of consciousness having no part in humanity's evolution, strictly speaking (because that consciousness when it reaches Them and enters the Sun, will be no longer human or "separate" from God), that they seem so far away and outside or beyond the Mars realm.

While seemingly outside, as we have shown these realms are really within our consciousness, for are we not traveling within towards the Sun Center of our being, and are not all ideas or centers of consciousness, including those of the seven planets, within our minds, all being centers of God's Mind, which includes all?

What we principally want you to see is that we are still contacting and are strongly influenced by the Mars realm, by its being next to the Earth realm on its outer side, while we are approaching the Venus realm on our inward journey. Through Venus' emotional states we must pass, taking with us and lifting up all its forces, and thereby acquiring the power to pass into and through the Mercury or mental realms, where in turn its forces when conquered will enable us to pass into the Sun realms. But all this time we are being aided by. the Jupiter, Saturn and Uranus forces brought to us by our Higher Selves, the Sons of God, in Their descent to us from the Sun Center of our being through those three realms, and whose forces are always available for our use.

In other words, in order to impress it more strongly on your mind, we will repeat, the Sun Center is within you, is the innermost center of your consciousness, and is not that Sun up in the sky that you think is the visible center of the Solar System. And every star and planet, including the Earth and all on it, as well as every other concept of your mind, are within your consciousness in realms reaching from the physical, the outermost, through an infinity of states of mind, soul and spirit, to the Sun itself, and then to the very Throne of God, the innermost center of your being. Think this over until you grasp it.

We have been trying to picture to you the most difficult thing possible—to make consciousness and forces appear to you as they are, and not what the human mind has been taught to believe them to be. In order to comprehend and accept what we have shown, you naturally will have to cast aside all former beliefs about the form and material side of planets, men, animals, etc., and try to view them as forces, the activities of consciousness deep within your own being; for all are actually in evidence there, hidden within your mind somewhere in the vast world of its consciousness, but always waiting and eager to come forth and serve you.

Let us recapitulate. The Sons of God, Who were responsible for all consciousness that makes up the planet Earth, when the time came for its redemption, descended from their Father God's Consciousness around His Throne in the Sun, into the Uranus realm, from there sending down into the darkness of the dense consciousness that was to become the Earth the first quickening impulse of Their life force; and began guiding that consciousness up through the various stages of the mineral kingdom. After which They descended a stage farther into Saturn's realm and from there sent a new and higher impulse of life force, directing the evolution of consciousness up through the vegetable kingdom. Then descending into Jupiter's realm They sent a still higher impulse of life and power, directing the unfolding consciousness up through the animal kingdom.

All of this took place in realms of consciousness, remember, and we are dealing only with ideas and thoughts in consciousness. So what seemed to be the mineral kingdom was only the darkest and densest state of consciousness, filled with thought creations of the basest and blackest sin and evil, to which no spiritual light could penetrate. In the vegetable stage of consciousness, the higher quickening impulse stimulated the life force therein to such effect that instinct was aroused the first sign of awakening life, in its reaction and endeavor to respond to and reach out for the light.

In the animal stage, instinct gradually became an actual desire for light, taking the form of hunger for food, in its effort to express the life forces pushing forth from within in response to the next quickening impulse, which in time developed eyes, ears, mouths, teeth, legs and claws, to enable it to seek, capture and to fight for what it desired to eat, possess or hold.

All these reactions of the desire forces of consciousness developed what are called animal characteristics, which to the human mind outpictured themselves as actual animals. But the only animals that ever existed are the animal forces of desire that were in long-forgotten lives allowed to rule without restraint. The yielding to these forces and then later learning their harmful effects and trying to free itself from them, caused the mind to picture them in consciousness as the animals we know today.

All of that lower stage of consciousness, before it was incorporated in the human soul, was acquired in the Mars realm, and consciousness is now engaged in freeing itself from the desires of the human nature, still largely animal, it is true, but more refined as it were, and which will always influence until the mind learns to rule both emotions and desire.

From all this you will learn that man is actually a god, a solar system in miniature, and "formed" in the image and likeness of God. You will also learn that man therefore is of course not flesh and blood, but is pure consciousness or spirit, a center of God's Mind, linked up with mighty forces that are waiting to lift him out of his limited consciousness into reahns far beyond his mortal comprehension. These forces are his forces, for they are within him; but he must learn to master them (and they, themselves, will help him do this, by combatting him until they develop his strength and wisdom) before he can wisely and constructively use them. When he can do this, he becomes more than man, for then he enters the realm where they dwell, as Lord and Conqueror, and they gladly become his servants.

From this you can see that you need not stay down in the selfish desire realms of Earth with the rest of humanity, any longer than you wish—knowing the truth about yourself. For you are a divine being, actually a Son of God—when you can let go of your sense of separation and unite your mind and consciousness with that of your Higher Self. Therefore the time will come when you can easily enter the Venus, Mercury, or even the Sun realms of consciousness at will; for when the Light of true Understanding is yours, the Light of The One Who is the Real You, you actually are in the Sun and of the Sun, the Sun of God.

So you now know that planets, the earth, and the Sun are but realms or states of consciousness within yourself and within all men and not places of habitation for men, human or super-human. Just so long as you think of yourself as inhabiting or wanting to journey to other planes of consciousness as a separate being, are you limiting yourself and keeping yourself separate from the Sun Center, your Father's Home in the

Kingdom. And do not confuse the seven Great Beings with the planets or realms of consciousness which They rule—for They are actually the Spirits around the Throne of God, through Whose states of consciousness (and with Their aid, which alone makes it possible) must all souls pass in their journey back within consciousness to their Father's Home.

Ponder over this before taking up what follows.

SPIRITUAL POVERTY

Did you ever try to interpret the spiritual meaning of the state or condition in which humanity finds itself today—the real cause, and do you know what alone will lift it out again into peace and harmony?

Yes, we know we already have given one explanation, —that it is because men have put all their trust in and dependence on money, on material things, on other men in high places; and because they have forgotten God. And this condition is to allow men to turn to these earthly sources for the help they need, and to show them that they can not get it there—for such can not or will not help them at the present time.

So a few are beginning to realize that this was brought upon them by their Higher Selves to turn them to God, as the only power that can now save them every other source having failed.

But this does not give the underlying spiritual cause. What does all this poverty, hardship and darkness symbolize? Let us try to explain. In order to do so we will illustrate with a letter from a dear one who was being taught the meaning of it, but who did not understand and wrote to us for an explanation.

"A few days before Christmas, 1932, my husband, my brother and I were in Los Angeles, walking up Seventh Street. As we neared the corner of Seventh and Flower Streets, I became very nervous and tired, the invisible holiness of persons was very strong about me, almost getting the best of me. We were to part at the corner. When we reached it I looked to the left; a tall thin man, very gentlemanly, was standing with his hat in his hand, 'begging.' The sight of him filled me with an agony of pity. I exclaimed, 'Oh, Hugh, look! that poor old man! Do give him something."

"He turned to look and at once acted on my suggestion. I was left standing but shaking beside my brother Henry. I was fumbling for a coin in my bag, when the thought came to me. 'I have already given on Broadway; so has Hugh; Henry has nothing to give (we are his only support, he being long out of work); give to him, so he can give.' I at once passed the money to him, saying, 'You give it to him, dear.'

"I was then alone, and looking across the street I saw another beggar, and on the far corner still another. My knees seemed as if they would not hold me. A taunting voice was saying, 'You give, and see what a holy thing you will witness.' I was afraid of this invisible holiness; I could not obey that voice; it seemed to be jeering at and pushing me.

"Oh! What was I to do? There were too many beggars; the condition was entirely beyond me.' flashed through my mind. Oh! I must overcome this awful terror. The thing must stop. i could not go up to any of them.

"I tried to brace myself. I feared I would fain. Then the huge buildings before me vanished; there was a picture poised in the air; many, many forms in long white robes, with heads uncovered, were standing in tall green grass, beautifully green, reaching to their knees, the center form resembling our dear Lord Jesus. As the picture vanished many more forms could be seen in the back' ground, all of course quite misty; the sky seemed full of them.

"Oh! I was so weak and faint I had to take my brother's arm. What had I seen? My God! My God! surely these must be the Master's sheep, starving in green pastures. Oh! What could I do to help? I who was so helpless.'

In very truth is the Father, through His Son, our Lord and Master and His servants, who stand waiting in fields filled with plenty, ready and anxious to supply our every need. And They are very close to us these dark times, even as was seen by our friend in the above letter. Think not because you can not see Them that this is not so. We must lift our minds and hearts to Them, or we cannot see and reach Them, or They us.

Those of His children who love and trust Him, He never lets lack any good or needed thing; but it is necessary that each be brought to that perfect faith and trust where there is no thought or question that every need is met even before it is felt. What many are going through now is the testing, strengthening and perfecting of His dear ones in such understanding.

Men have for so long been led to believe that the good things of the material life produced by science, and the great intellectual advancement of the race, alone are necessary and suffice; while they have been fed so little of real spiritual food by the hundreds of thousands of churches organized to provide it, that their souls today are actually starving. Souls have to be fed, as well as bodies, and unless they receive nourishing food, exactly as is the case with their bodies, they starve, or suffer from mal-nutrition, feel depleted, depressed, discouraged, and the spiritual life which would sustain them drops to the lowest ebb. Who will say that mankind is not in such a condition today, with the exception of a comparatively few?

We showed you in the first article herein where the bulk of humanity is at its present stage of evolution on the higher desire planes of the Earth realm. But we see that all men are now going through a -most trying period, where the Forces of Light connected with their higher natures are preparing to free them from the dark' ness of their lower animal natures that would engulf them and prevent their taking the new step forward in evolution that awaits those who are ready. And there are a goodly number who are to be lifted entirely out of the darkness into the light of pure Spirit; while all humanity will be advanced one stage farther toward the Venus realm of consciousness.

That is what the great number of our Brothers of Light, seen by our friend above mentioned and by many others, are waiting for for those who show any signs of seeking spiritual help. All are lovingly watched over and all members of humanity, no matter on what plane of life— those on the lowest and darkest as well as those on the highest spiritual planes, will be advanced to higher planes by the quickening power of Spirit now being poured down into the earth consciousness by the Angels of Light and Love, Who have descended close to Earth for that sole purpose.

PERSONAL PERFECTION

Because physical health and perfection are so much desired and sought after, we wish to present a few thoughts for your consideration. At the same time and for the same reason, because of their close connection, can be considered the desire for physical comfort and the good things of life, all consequent upon the possession of plenty of money.

Not that health and money are to be despised by those trying to live the spiritual life; although in India they are so regarded, and a devotee actually gives away all he possesses, when he starts out to find union with God; he renounces home, family and friends, and thereafter lives wholly on alms, considering not at all his health in so doing.

In the light of all that have been teaching, that the physical body and all in the outer world are mere illusions—are but creations of the "separate" mortal mind and exist only in that mind,, and that man's real body and world are all good and all perfect now and therefore do not have to be sought and striven for, can you not see what desiring and seeking for that goodness and perfection in the physical implies and actually does for you?

Think! You who are seeking union with your Higher Self, and at the same time are desiring freedom from that weakness or inharmony of the flesh and from that condition of lack and limitation that is holding you back from the peace and harmony you crave.

Remember the Law: Whatever you think and hold in your consciousness as being so outmanifests itself.

Then if you are trying to free yourself from something, are you not just as surely thinking of and seeing that thing as being so and thus giving it power over you, as though you were deliberately trying to create it?

What is wrong then, and how can you be free from the ill-health and the limited conditions which you are compelled to endure at the present time, despite your earnest prayers and desire for deliverance from them? It seems almost impossible of a solution, does it not?

But there is a solution, and you have been shown it time and time again. It is only you who have made health and money such a serious problem that you have chronic ill-health and find money evading your constant efforts to secure it, that we are talking to now. We have hundreds of such writing us who need to -see this great truth and to learn the lesson we will try to make plain herein.

Health of body can only come from harmony of mind. Harmony of mind can come only from knowing the truth. And knowing the truth can only come from letting go with your mind and allowing the truth to penetrate beneath the surface of mind into the soul, your true consciousness, where alone it lives and causes you to express and act the truth.

By that we mean that you must stop trying to do anything of yourself, must chiefly stop desiring what you lack; and instead must simply let go, get quiet, and allow the life and health of that perfect body in the invisible to flow forth and express itself. Flow forth from where? From your soul, which is the real you, living now and always in your perfect body within.

Let that truth penetrate through your mind to your soul, and thus open the door so that the real you can come forth.

Yes, it is as simple as that—when you can once get your mind to let go, so your soul can act.

And even as your soul lives in a perfect body, so does it live in a perfect world (of consciousness, remember) where all that the Father hath is everywhere present and always available for .its use. There you need nothing, for the need always creates its own fulfillment, like air rushing into a vacuum. It will be exactly the same here (in your mind's consciousness) when you can altogether link your mind with your soul consciousness, by the mind's simply knowing this truth, and letting - fulfillment flow through immediately into expression.

But the trouble is, you say, in the mind's not wholly letting go, and in not perfectly linking its consciousness with its soul knowing.

Well, if you know the trouble, why not work with it until you have conquered it? That is the only way you can get anywhere. And the remarkable thing about it is that you will need to do nothing. When your soul really sees that the mind wants to give up, then it begins to act and does all the work for you. Your part is but to co-operate with it by letting it.

From all this you can see how foolish it is to desire anything in order to possess it physically or personally. It only separates you farther from your soul and closes the door, preventing the very thing from coming through into expression that your soul was seeking to manifest through you.

If when you had first felt the need, instead of strongly desiring what you needed, you had immediately got quiet and connected your consciousness with its source, the door would have opened wide, and by this time your own good would be manifesting freely in your life.

X. PROVE Me Now, Saith The Lord"

PAPER No. 44. AUGUST, 1932

The time has come for you to know more of the realities of life. So we now ask you to try to realize the life that as a soul and a disciple of Christ you are actually living in the soul realm of the Kingdom—that realm where are consciously and always when your body sleeps and when you are free to give all your attention to that life and your work there.

As you now read, forget that you are in a body of flesh, but are truly living in a younger and a beautiful spiritual body, perfect in its health and strength, for it is formed in the image and likeness of God.

And you are living likewise with many others in similar bodies in a beautiful and perfect world beyond all comparison to the world of physical matter; for it is the real and ideally perfect of what the outer world would be—if man had available and was using all of his divine faculties and powers and was in no way limited by lack of understanding of what was pure beauty, goodness, loveliness, gentleness, brotherliness, selflessness and truth, and was therefore always living and expressing these qualities.

This may be a little difficult for you to imagine now, bet a; go on you may find yourself in a consciousness where all these things will seem natural and an actual part your being.

Therefore try to see yourself living in this perfect world in a home truly suited to your innate. nature, satisfying your every cultural and aesthetic taste and need, and in social relations with others happily leaving nothing to be desired, There everyone has his own work and is always busy at it, for he or she fills a perfect part a perfect plan, where the loving desire and purpose Dt each to fulfill his or her part in keeping the whole in perfect order, is supreme.

Naturally then you are working in closest co-operation with all others to that end. Each one there being a producer, plenty is provided for everyone needs; for as each one produces a large surplus above his own needs. such surplus is stored and kept available for the use of others. Because of this, each one thus being a worker and producer, there is always a big surplus, despite the fact that no one works more than a few hours a day, or two or three days a week, leaving plenty of leisure for study and time for service.

Try to realize that our life as souls in the soul realm is life—is our real life, the one here in the outer being but a sorry and sordid expression of it, due to man´s wrong teachings and beliefs concerning God, his self and life's purpose for him. There we live a far more natural and full life, complete in every department and detail, so ideally perfect that it is beyond the capacity of our human minds to conceive it.

Let us tell you the wonderful part of that life. We seem to be living in a very atmosphere of love, knowing it both as the Father's love and His Consciousness. For from that atmosphere we derive everything we are and need. Let us see if we can explain.

There everyone knows that God is All in all, that it is in His Consciousness we live, move and have our being. We know therefore that His Consciousness is our Consciousness and what life we have is His life and consequently that all of His Wisdom, Power and Love comprise our very nature: that from what you would call the air—is supplied everything we need. For do we not breathe in that air --the Breath of God's Love, do we not live in it? Then is it not our life?

There of course we need no food to sustain us, for God's Love-life as we breathe it in is our life, our sustenance and -supply. And of course that Life provides and maintains us in perfect health and strength, even as His Love-consciousness inspires our every thought, word and act. For being Consciousness and therefore being one with Him, His Will is always being expressed through us—is our will; for there, there is no other will, even as there is no other life or consciousness.

From this you can see there is no self, no possible sense of separation; for all being of one mind and one will, we are all part of an All which rules and is our life.

God's Love thus being the animating essence and motive power of our life, service or the doing of God's Will is always uppermost in our minds. And so we spend most of our time, when not engaged in study and in the little necessary work that is our part, in helping others —-in teaching children or our younger brothers in Spirit, when such work is apportioned us by Those in charge but principally in watching over, inspiring and those still in the flesh—at night, when our bodies are asleep. For even our souls have reached this oneness of consciousness, and as all the children al God are also a part of His Consciousness, we can never rest until everyone still wandering in the darkness self and of fancied separation from Him brought into the Light of His Love, that they too may partake of and be consciously part of His Love-life.

Also, may we tell you, many of us have so trained and disciplined our human expressions that during the daytime in the ordinary routine of our presence and guidance is not required, leaving us free in the soul realms to do many deeds of service, visiting dear   ones   and   others needing help, inspiring, encouraging and strengthening them in the problems confronting them. When our presence is required with our human personalities, we are always there to direct, caution or help as the need is. Many are beginning to realize that they are much more than what their human minds have pictured themselves to be: that they are souls living in a higher consciousness directing life and activities of their human expressions, which are but instruments they are developing, disciplining and training in preparation for the time when they can take full possession of and live their lives, do their will, and be their Real Selves in them, without let or "hindrance of any kind, even as we have pictured to you they are now living as souls in the kingdom.

A few are actually conscious of living in two worlds at the same time, their soul faculties having been quickened to the extent that they see and hear on both planes.

We have already mentioned that the veil is growing thin between the two worlds and it will not be long before all true disciples of Christ – those who have proved themselves-- will be fully conscious their soul life. What we are all going through at the present time is the proving process, where we are having shown up to our human minds every quality of the lower self that still stands in and which must be eliminated, for such qualities form the veil hiding from our minds the true world of the Kingdom.

When the veil is finally lifted, which will be only when the Divine Union takes place and the lower and separate self is no more, all of its forces having been lifted up, transmuted and given over wholly to the Christ's use, center of consciousness will be transferred from your outer or human mind to the innermost of your heart, in the soul realm, and you will be living in your true consciousness as a Son of God in the real world of Kingdom.

Then the outer world will seem as a dream, unreal and visionary, even as to you now seems the inner world of the spirit. Then you will know that the real world is almost the exact opposite of what you now see in the outer world; that it is all good and all perfect, as compared to 'the dark, evil, hard, limited and imperfect conditions now manifest everywhere to your outer senses.

When this veil is finally lifted for all which will be with the coming of the Lord "in the air," then you can see how those who are left will find themselves in their true homes in the realms. All evil minded ones will be in the dark realms of the lowest and outermost regions of consciousness where selfishness and greed altogether rule. the masses of mankind, those who are neither good or bad and in whom the spirit still sleeps, will find themselves in the intermediate realms of the astral or mental, according to the growth of their souls. In other words they will be just where their souls are now, in those soul realms of consciousness where they belong and truly affinitize.

It will be exactly the same as if they had died and they no longer had physical bodies. But then death will for with the coming of the Lord and His Legions—the Sons of Light, Their vibrations will be so powerful that only those who have proven themselves to His true disciples can live in and endure them. their physical bodies will simply disappear with their human, "separate" consciousness, even as darkness disappears before the light: or rather their consciousness will remain in the lower vibration of which it is an art, while the heavenly consciousness descends and possesses the earth and all able to abide in it.

Thus will the Kingdom, which we described in the first part of this article and that before was invisible except to the spiritual sight, become visible to every "living soul" on earth and will be their natural world and its life their natural life. Although as we have shown, many before that time comes will have consciously entered the Kingdom, will have dissolved the; veil and will be living in what seems to be two worlds, even though their consciousness is then centered in the real world of the soul, and the outer is known to be unreal.

Our part is to help as many as possible to make the change as quickly as may be—to transfer their centers of consciousness from the mind to the soul, so that they may from then on be working consciously with their Brothers in the Kingdom for the advent of the New Day, when true world of the spirit shall be on earth even as it is in Heaven.

MONEY

We will now take up the consideration of what is money. The dictionary says money is "any material which by agreement serves as a common medium of exchange and measure of value in trade.

But let us see if we cannot bring out the spiritual idea, the real meaning and purpose of money; for as you must realize money is not used or needed in Heaven. Then it must be a substitute for something that is used there, but which man either cannot or will not use here in his dealings with his fellow men. Think on this for a bit and see if it must not be true.

First let us consider why money is not used or needed in Heaven. Must it not be because there everyone loves and trusts each other and wants to help and do unto others as they would be clone by? Is that the case here? Then because of this money must have been invented as some, thing needed that could serve as a substitute and could be invested with a value that everyone would accept far what was being sold or exchanged.

But that not being necessary in Heaven, what there took the place of money? Let us see.

Did we not show you that in the Kingdom we ever live in an atmosphere of Love; that that atmosphere is God's Love, and it is so wonderful an atmosphere that from it we derive everything we need and. are, sustains, strengthens and gives us our life—is our life, and it not only supplies us with the necessary food to sustain that life, but inspires our every thought, word and act?

Can you not see that God's Love is our sole support, supply and sufficiency in all things at all times—that It is there what men have made money to be here?

Ponder on this until you see how true it is and then see if you can glimpse what is necessary before can be to you what it really should be, and not what you and your fellowmen have made it to be.

Take a coin or a bill out of your pocket and hold it in your hand, and try to see it as a symbol of God's Love. That may seem difficult at first; but, as every manifest thing is a symbol of an idea, you of course have to put all other ideas formerly held about money out of your mind, and must not even see the coin or bill but must look right through it and try see, or rather feel, God's Love flowing to you from out the symbol.

Persist in trying this until you do feel that Love, and then note the wonderful things that follow—the impressions and feelings that illumine mind and heart-—the realization that God and money are most intimately related, and that God does want you to have the abiding evidence and the fullest sufficiency of what money really represents—His blessed Love and the accompanying Understanding and Power that belong to every one His children.

What will this mean to you? Think! If you can feel that Love, and thereby' act. the Understanding, then, dear one, you connect your mind and its consciousness with God's Consciousness and through the channel of the of the idea you are holding in your hand, the door is opened wide and there is no longer anything to prevent the reality of what the symbol truly represents from flowing to you in rich abundance —-for you have tapped the Source, the Spiritual Idea that brought the symbol into being.

But beware of how you use this wonderful truth. We have given it to you in order that you may know the reality back of the symbol, and no longer will look upon money as the monster which men have made it.

Anyone who attempts to use this truth for the getting of money for purely selfish purposes will learn to his everlasting regret that spiritual truths and forces cannot be used for the benefit of self, and that a heavy penalty must be paid for every such attempt. On the other hand, those who seek through this truth to prove the real meaning of money, as God's Love, and thereby to come closer Into oneness with Him, helping thus to eliminate self and its desires utterly, will find themselves invested with a Knowing and a consequent Power, that is inconceivable to a mind still seeking money for itself or anything that money can buy.

Money or the possession of money has given to man a fraudulent power that will surely bring about his own destruction. His love of money with his false idea of money's purpose have grown to such distorted proportions and have brought about such a perversion of its original purpose that the destruction of both money and all who thus misuse it, cannot help but follow; for they are deliberately misusing God's Love, the most powerful force in the universe. Instead of using Its symbol for the helping and blessing of humanity, man has allowed himself to be enticed into seeking it purely for selfish or personal ends, either to provide for his material needs or to build for himself a power and prestige among his fellows whereby he can exercise authority over them, and compel them to create for him more money and power.

Just think of man's perverting the visible symbol of God's Love in such a way, and the penalty he must pay for so doing! Then think of what it might be if man could use money always and only as a tangible expression of God's Love flowing freely through him! We wonder if that could possibly be! What a different world we would then live in!

Let us give you a word of caution. Do not be surprised or dismayed if the false value and power money now possesses is altogether taken from it in the near future and that possibly money will become worthless. For if the Kingdom is to come down and be on earth and money is not needed in the Kingdom, the destroying of money's power will   be.   a   clear sign of the near approach of that great Coming. And remember, all of the old order--everything built for selfish ends or even to maintain the system of competition of individuals against individuals, industries against industries, countries against countries; which means practically all our institutions, commercial, industrial, financial, educational and even religious must go, and will utterly vanish from our midst, before the -kingdom can be established here and we be a part of it.

Therefore begin now and make your peace with money: learn always to see and know it as an expression of God's Love and Power, for it is the Power that can make you anything you will --when your will is united with His Will by such seeing and knowing.

God, Who is All in all, Who is therefore all that you are and all that money, is, when your mind and its ideas are thus united with His on the money idea you are in its vibration, are on its wave-length—to use a radio term; and it must flow to you from the All of His Mind, as long as you keep the channel of your mind open by a perfect seeing and knowing.

Then whenever money comes to you or you give it to others, always see and feel it as a direct evidence of God s Love that you are either receiving or giving. Let your love flow forth to God in return to God Who is within both you and your brother –Who is All in all-- Who is the Love which always blesses, when we see Him as He IS.

We have given you these truths help you in these dark hours of trial and tribulation. Praise God and thank Him daily, hourly, for His many blessings. Prove to Him now that you are worthy of what He has given you and of all that He is waiting to deliver to you.

"PROVE ME NOW"

In the July Paper and in the above you are provided with much food for thought, nay much food for your soul, which when fully digested and assimilated will pre pare you for what follows.

You have been shown the only way of release from the "Depression," in which the whole world is now involved,—that you must lift your mind entirely from it and require it to stay in your true consciousness, that of a Son of God. We have shown that in order to do this you must deliberatively and persistently practice-thinking, speaking and acting as a Son of God, until you are actually living in your true consciousness in the Kingdom and there is no longer a lower and a higher self, but only You, in your Christ Consciousness, seeing God in all things and knowing your Oneness with Him.

If you are now practicing working from this Consciousness, then you have digested and are assimilating the food supplied, and through the Grace of the Christ Spirit within the power is being give you to be your True Self on earth as well as in Heaven. No, this is not impossible. It is your Divine heritage and nature and it but awaits your recognition and acceptance to manifest here and now. But it cannot manifest until you assume that it is so, and begin to act accordingly.

What do we mean? That not until you begin to assume your true nature, will the power start to flow through quickening in you the true consciousness enabling you to act as a Son of God.

We are trying so to inspire you with the truth of your real nature and power as a soul and Son of God being ever ready to come forth into expression, that you will begin now to assume your Sonship, will go about in that consciousness, and will prove to your human mind that You and Your Father are One and all that He is you are.

Does not the Christ Self of you always say to your human mind, "If ye abide in Me, and My words abide in you, ye shall ask what ye will and it shall be done unto you?" Surely you can see that means if it abides in Your Christ Consciousness and Your words abide in its consciousness, they will inspire and direct all its thinking, speaking and acting, and it will no more need anything, for You will provide it with ail things, even as You are now provided in Heaven.

We know that you cannot get your human mind to abide continually in your consciousness at first, but not unless you persist and require it to do so more and more each day, can it get the habit of so doing. And we know that you cannot get -it to abide at all unless you have brought it to a more or less clear realization that you are its True Self, and it and its personal self are nothing, can do nothing, can have nothing. only as You give them the power to be, to do and to have anything.

But you are supposed to have brought it to such realization through the proving of the many teachings given it in the past. And so you should fully understand and be able to respond to what we now shall say. Consider carefully every word.

If you truly realize that God is All in all, and that then He must be you, by holding to that realization and starting to act as a Son or expression of God, God will through you, and His Power and Grace will flow through and enable you to do anything you essay to do.

We do not ask you to believe this, We do ask you to try it --to prove it-- to show your God-self that you are ready to put yourself and your instrument wholly in Hi; hands, so that He can empower you as He wills.

Is it unnatural that as His Son you should assume to be like Him and to use His Power as a God? Did He not form you in His image and likeness so that He can express the fullness of His nature through you? Then why limit Him any longer by deeming yourself less than you are a "Son of the Living God," and "Joint Heir with Christ?"

The time will soon be when you must assume your true nature. When we tell you that by assuming to be what you actually are the proofs must follow, you will see how close you are to the reality of your Divine nature without knowing it,

All that you have to do is to know that God is ALL is you, is every faculty, power and quality of your nature; is your life, your mind, your body, every part of your self—that there is no weakness, limitation or imperfection because He is all that you are. Think on this long and earnestly until you get it.

Then you must likewise know that He, being ALL, is everybody and everything that is: that they are therefore all good and perfect, as expressions of Him, despite what your human mind tells you; and that there is nothing else but Him. You must hold to this truth, though all the world deny it. Can you see what that will gradually do to your consciousness? It will make you soon to see, hear, feel, smell, taste, think, believe, know. BE God only. He will then fill your consciousness to the exclusion of all else, and thus will be your SELF, the only Self there is. Ah, dear one, if We can only get you to see this—to prove it for yourself! What a glorious blessing will be yours!

When you can by doing this thus make yourself as a GOD—not a God but as God: of the same nature and substance—then by this knowing the natural flow of God-expression will take place and you will begin to understand you are "under grace,"--will taste of the unutterable sweets of the Christ Natures Then you will find that you will "decree a thing and it shall come to pass" and many wonderful evidences of the God powers working through you will follow.

You will not have to visualize or imagine it, for as it truly exists in the kingdom you see it there with spiritual, the eyes of knowing. Assuming the Divine as God—you always see the perfect whereas formerly you saw only the imperfect.

From the standpoint of assumption, you will see health your natural state and disease non existent. You will cease trying to get rid of disease as a reality and will know yourself as a Son of God living in perfect health and harmony of Spirit. One moment of this realization and disease has vanished into nothingness, for the Perfect Self is thereby revealed and made manifest.

From the standpoint of assumption, you will gain the actual, concrete results you failed to accomplish by imagination and visualization. Are you afraid to follow the steps of the Master and to assume your Divine rights so that they can come forth into manifestation? Are you afraid to accept the results of consciously accepting your birthright?

"The worm of the dust" finally discovers that he can do nothing to change of better himself, for he is a product of the dual belief in good and evil. Working with the body and personality, trying to perfect them, is exactly the same.

No matter what you have been, have done, or have left undone, when the Christ within is fully recognized as your True Self, all former limitations pass away. Thousands of sincere souls, seeking the light, have spent years trying to better the conditions of the "worm of the dust" trying to make "John Smith" a better man, healthier, richer or happier; but have accomplished little, or nothing. The worm cannot change except from within. The caterpillar of itself can never become butterfly. A complete change has to take place— a transformation. What accomplishes it?

Only by yielding to the mind; the will of the life within, can the change take place. The caterpillar instinctively knows this and lets nature have its way. Only man rebels, interferes and interposes his own will and his ideas. But when the Holy Spirit is born in the beginning of a change takes place in his nature; and when the spiritual man grows to maturity; the Christ, a Son of God, emerges from the cocoon of the personality and its cloak of protection is cast off.

So will it be with you when you assume your true nature. You are now as the butterfly ready to break through and rise out of the cocoon: but like the butterfly you must make the effort, must respond to the urge of the Christ-life within-—when It will give you the power, not only to break through your flimsy shell of self but to rise and fly to heights undreamed of. Then your neve will be so far removed from the old, that the old will be as a dream. "The former things shall pass away—they shall be remembered no more, neither shall they come to mind." Then as a Son of the Living God, living and moving in your new kingdom of expression, all fears and worries—the cause and effect of the "John Smith" drop away and be even as the cocoon of the butterfly.

"Be still and know, I AM, God" then takes on a new meaning: Be still and assume the glories of the new estate. Assume them in the secret place, easily, naturally —-the power to do so will be given you, remember; assume them and rest in the quiet knowing of your True Self. In that knowing you will see nothing, hear nothing, be aware of nothing in the without; but you will see all, hear all, and know all in the within.

Be still and serenely assume the God given qualities and hide them deep within silence of your new consciousness. Then they will burst forth when needed as glorious expressions of your freed being.

Be not afraid; it is I"—"I, who stand at the door and knock. I am always there, awaiting your recognition and letting Me in, waiting to give you of all that I am and have, to use in the expression of the Christ Self which you then will be in full consciousness. Identify yourself now with Me and be at peace.

Prove me now, saith the Lord of Hosts, (and see) if I will not open you the windows of heaven and pour you out a blessing that there shall be no room enough to receive it" Malachi 3.10

We are glad to credit a number of thoughts in the above to Walter Lanyon, taken from a most inspiring article entitled ASSUMPTION, in the Metaphysical News, Seattle, June 8th issue.

Xi. THE SUBSTANCE OF THINGS HOPED FOR

PAPER No. 45, SEPTEMBER, 1932

IN THE August Paper, entitled ' 'Prove Me Now, Saith the Lord," were shown you some glorious truths; one especially, that by assuming your real nature as a Son of God divine activities would naturally follow. We are hoping that many of you are beginning to know and to assume your divine powers and possibilities.

In this article we will help you to prove some of these powers—those of you who have the courage to venture beyond the realm of visible "facts" and to trust all to the of things not seen. In other words, we are going to test and help you build up your faith.

In the 11th chapter of his Epistle to the Hebrews, in the first verse of the St. James version, Paul says, 'Faith is the substance of things hoped for, the evidence of things not seen." In the Revised version it is given, "Faith is the assurance of things hoped for, a conviction of things not seen." While in the Emphatic Diaglott, containing the original Greek text, it reads, "Faith is the basis of things hoped for, a conviction of things unseen."

We like the, first one best, as more clearly expressing what we feel faith to be, and as Paul probably meant it —if we could know his exact meaning.

First realize that there is an actual substance with which faith works. Of course that substance is not visible to the sight, but it is none the less a real and tangible substance to the mind, once it learns consciously to work with it through faith.

Which means then that somewhere in the invisible there is a substance, that with our thought, through faith, we can mould, shape and form into conditions and things, and bring them forth into visibility. Think this over until you see that it is exactly what faith accomplishes.

Now most of you through faith a great many times in one form or another have accomplished just that: although you may not have done it consciously or purposely. But it was your faith nevertheless that brought it to pass. Surely then, if it has been accomplished thus unconsciously, it can be done consciously any number of times-when the same identical use of faith is always followed.

Let us search into and examine this invisible substance that faith is said to be, and see if we can learn its real nature and the secret of its power, so that i.ve can use it consciously and can accomplish it what evidently is Intended every disciple of Christ shall accomplish. For did not Jesus say to His disciples, when they asked Him why they could not cure the epileptic, "Because of your little faith, for verily I say unto you, If se have faith as mustard seed, ye shall say unto this mountain, Remove hence to yonder place; and it shall remove, and nothing shall be impossible unto you." Mat. 17 :20 R.V.

There are many stories told of what has been accomplished by faith, you all know the wonderful things Paul tells in the 11th Chapter of Hebrews. Jesus credits most of the healings He performed to the faith of those healed and blessed, saying ' 'According to faith, be it done unto you. "Thy faith hath made thee whole" "O woman, great is thy faith; be it done unto thee even as thou wilt." "Thy faith hath saved thee.", etc.

Now all these things that were accomplished were done by visioning clearly in the invisible the thing sought (with no Signs of it apparent in the outer) and believing it was so or it could be done and would manifest.

Try to realize this fully before we proceed, for you must see that the real work is done in the invisible, and that what you can clearly see in the invisible can be made, to become visible in the outer—through the action of faith.

YOU have all heard or read many times what was just stated, and many of you have often tried to prove it, with only partial or most unsatisfactory results. And of course all wish to know why you failed, and the sure way always to succeed.

First know that there is a definite law of faith, and that it works just as surely as any law of mathematics or of electricity, when clearly understood and correctly used.

Secondly, know that you are working just as truly with an invisible substance that is moulded and shaped by your thought, as does the potter work with clay that he moulds and shapes with his hands.

Thirdly, when something is visioned clearly—that is, is seen as a FINISHED thing in the invisible, if it remains finished and accomplished in your mind with no slightest doubt or question but that it will appear speedily in the outer, --in accordance with the law through such a faith it will so appear.

With these things fixed in your consciousness we Will now examine into the right way of working with this substance. Of course by your thinking you have been unconsciously moulding and shaping this substance from the beginning—even from the cradle. Witness the results in your body, your environment and your affairs. Yes, they are what you have thought them. into being you cannot get away from it; it is the law

—what you think, you are. Which implies also that what you think, your world and all in it are.

That means of course that you, your body, your environment, your affairs, your world and all your fellowmen. are what you see with your mortal eyes and believe to be in your mortal mind. They are what you have thought and thereby made them be-- but they are such only to your mortal understanding, or as they appear to your mortal mind.

Do you get the distinction? What they are, they are only in the outer or visible world, or as they appear to your physical senses and are believed to be by your mortal mind. But they are not so in the invisible world—in the realm of Reality.

Learning from this that your thinking only moulds this invisible substance into the form and shape of your beliefs, you can see how important it is to have only correct beliefs. For beliefs are but thoughts filled with the substance of faith, either already or about to be manifested in your body, world or affairs. And they may be altogether wrong beliefs, causing you untold inharmony, suffering and hardship. Witness your belief in disease, poverty, death and all of those inharmonious things now manifesting in your life —all of them lies and having no existence in the invisible realm of God's kingdom— His Consciousness.

(Go back over this and study carefully every statement until you grasp clearly its meaning. Then you are ready for what follows.)

From all of the above it would appear that the only way understandingly to use this power of thinking is to get back into the Invisible and to work wholly from there. We of course can do that only in consciousness; and by going back into our soul consciousness --back into Silence. where we can shut out all sense of the outer with its claims and concerns of self --we there can glimpse and may even get a clear vision of that perfect world within where are no inharmonies, no lies, no lack or limitation of any good, or needed thing.

You have had proved to you there is such a world, even if something within had not long ago convinced you there is where the I AM, the Real You lives. Therefore when in the Silence of your soul, it should not be difficult to let the heavens of your consciousness unfold and this perfect world appear to you inner vision.

Do you perceive what we mean? In that consciousness what appears is the real--it is not mere Imagination, you are then in a realm where the real and the true now appear and can be seen, for all mortal mind´s beliefs have been left without. You are now a soul in your real consciousness—the real of that of which the mortal mind is but a limited outer expression, and when you leave behind all wrong and limiting mortal beliefs—self´s creations—and open your consciousness to what appears from within, can you not perceive that what comes to you must be what exists there in this invisible realm of the real?

If this is clear, you can grasp that in this consciousness the. I AM, the Real You, naturally will bring to your attention the things He wishes you to know and to express, and as a disciple you are concerned only that, and doing His will, having learned that He always knows best and always purposes manifesting the best for you, as fast as you are able to use it in His service.

AT THIS point we wish to emphasize that it is always the self that wants things --that tries to make demonstrations—for self's use or its fancied needs: not realizing that the I AM, the Father, always knows best our needs and will always provide them when self and its wants are not in the way. On the other hand, it is the soul, thinking and working in conjunction with its Father within, that always wants to express the fullness of its true life as a Son of God, to manifest in the outer the abundance and perfection of all the good things every where present in that inner life in the Kingdom, ---but it cannot, because of self's interfering by wanting all for its oven personal use. Stop and realize how true this is.

Therefore, if you would learn rightly to use the power and substance of faith, always remember these two things:

(l) that whatever comes to you thus in the Silence from the Innermost consciousness actually exists in this invisible realm of the soul:

(2) That it is brought to your attention by your Higher Self purposely for you to know, and to bring forth, if needed, under His direction; for He knows best what He wants you to do with it. This means, of course, that self can have no part in it; that you are to wait upon Him and to obey Him only in what He directs you to do.

Do you realize what this signifies? If you truly believe what has just been said, and have perfect trust in Him— that is, if your faith is as a grain of mustard seed, the same power that makes what is in the mustard seed grow quickly into a tree, will cause what you see in the invisible of the soul realm to grow; and come forth quickly in the visible or outer world. For the same law that directs the growth of the idea or thought of a mustard tree hidden in the mustard seed and planted in the soil (or soul) of earth, likewise directs the idea or thought planted in the invisible soul substance of your mind; and when it is nourished and watered by perfect faith and trust, it must come forth into evidence, as Paul claims.

Think for a moment of the soil as the soul substance of earth, and how everything that lives, when *"planted" in the* soil, grows and thrives—if the soil is fertile and there is plenty of water and sunshine. This includes man and animals, for do not they have to be "planted" in the right kind of soil—that fitted to their nature—and be properly nourished by it to grow and thrive perfectly?

What is it in the soil that makes everything grow? Is it not this invisible soul substance, the real substance of the earth? What would the earth be with its sand and rock without the soul of itself, this essence of life always existing beneath the surface of the visible in the invisible substance that supports, animates and gives being to the material nature? And if hidden in that soil of earth is what gives life and visibility to all appearing upon it, can you not now see how hidden in the soil or mortal consciousness of your mind, there is the invisible but very real substance of your soul—that which gives life, form and visibility to all conditions and things appearing to your outer senses? Think this over until you see how wonderfully true it is.

NOW, of what practical use is all this to you? You are anxious to know just how to make the invisible become visible. But We are not to tell you how, in so many words. For that anxiety is purely of the self and it must not be gratified. But above we have given you the law, and how it works for those who work with it, and those who are truly in earnest about knowing and proving the law—under the direction of the Higher Self, will discover the true meaning back of the words and will be shown just how to apply it in all needed ways.

Therefore, if you would discover that meaning, read over carefully all that has been stated, and when something within causes you to halt and ponder over certain words, go within, in the silence of your soul, and wait and listen for all that is told and shown you there—and you will richly rewarded.

But we said at the beginning that would test and help you build up your faith, and we will now try to help prove the Lord, that you may see how He pours upon those who truly love and trust Him the blessings promised.

We have said and have impressed it upon you in many ways about letting go and living yourself in perfect trust to God Some of you have had many wonderful evidences of His loving care, and are amazed at how, with no work for months and no actual income, you have always been provided for and seemingly you are better off and happier than when you had plenty of money but did not have these truths and your present faith to strengthen and sustain you. Such have had very real proof that God is your support, your supply, your sufficiency in all things.

But such think truly that it is not His will or purpose that they remain long in such condition. They gladly remain, however, until they have learned all the lessons to be gained therefrom, knowing when their faith and trust have become perfect. and fully established they will automatically rise out of such condition or limited consciousness into their true place in the Kindom: such faith and trust having become the knowing of their Higher Selves that all the Father hath is theirs, and that He and they are One. And such knowing more than anything else helps to bring the Divine Union that awaits every disciple of Christ.

What is that desperate problem you are now facing, which must me bet and handled, or dire disaster seemingly will follow?

Is it a mortgage that must be met, a payment to be made, something to be accomplished by a given date, that in your limited consciousness seems impossible of realization? What is to be done?

First, you must get quiet, must retire into the Silence of your soul, leaving that limited consciousness altogether in the outer where it belongs. Command powerfully the forces of your mind to "Be still and know, I am, God," and mean that they shall obey. Then wait until there is perfect stillness.

When all is at peace within and nothing from without is in evidence, turn your thought to your problem, but unconcernedly and impersonally. Then wait, with your thought thus focused upon it, and see what comes. Be patient. Let nothing disturb you. Just wait.

Soon may come a definite impression or suggestion from within, indicating a new mode of action, something you had not thought of before, You may then make a silent query such as: "Father is this what, Thou desirest me to do?"

The chances are you will feel a strong affirmative response from within. If not, wait for another impression, and even ask, "Father, show me what is Thy will and purpose for me." And then wait calmly and confidently for a reply. Which may come as a strong impression or suggestion that you will feel is His reply.

Or soon after turning your thought to your problem, definite words may push forth from within, such as:

Why do you worry? Am I not here? Do I, your Loving Father, not know your need? Am I not able to supply your every need—I who brought you to this place, to this seemingly desperate situation, simply to show you the futility of seeking outer help, and to cause you earnestly to seek Me, to long for Me and My help; and then to bring you humbly and trustingly to Me, that I can prove to you My Love and My Power, and that I am an ever-present help in time of trouble?"

In both of such cases, you should immediately say, 'Father, I thank Thee, and accept this proof of Thy love, I put myself wholly in Thy hands, and will follow faithfully Thy every leading. I know that if I do my part, Thou wilt do Thine. I ask humbly that Thou Give me the faith and the strength of purpose to do whatever I am shown."

Then go about your business calmly and happily for there will come with this experience a peace and a confidence that will be truly uplifting. This attitude of mind you must hold continually, despite what appears in the outer or what others say.

If there is a date on which must be accomplished what is needed, let that not concern you. For with the Father time is not, and every good and needed thing is ever available and always present in the invisible Kingdom of God´s Mind. All you need do is to see it as He sees it— already accomplished, knowing it will appear in the outer before the time needed.

It may not appear until the last day, nay, the last hour, or even moment; but always it will appear on time, if your faith is great enough.

Study over the foregoing carefully, until you see how by doing exactly as is shown, you build up a quality of faith that is invincible, and which must be your faith before you can work in full conjunction with the Father´s will and purpose for you. Think of what that means—when you can do this, and of the blessings that must follow.

******

And now read slowly the next article, meditating on each sentence until you see how wonderfully it confirms the main truths in what is stated above.

SIMPLICITY

(From "The Spirit Spake")
THOU shalt preach the Name of Jesus Christ ONLY.

Enter not into the maze of sophistry or thou wilt find thou canst not extricate thyself therefrom. The Lord Jesus is the beginning and End of all things.

Feed thy brother with Divine Simplicity, so shalt thou bring him nearer unto Me. Say not unto him, "Lo! There are seven wonders. Rather say unto him, "The Lord is here. and Heaven is within thee."

Cling to the rock that is higher than thee—--the Ever lasting Foundation of knowledge, Trouble not. God has solved the problems of Eternity.

Why questionest thou all these things? The Father giveth thee Light as thou art able to receive it. Ye are the Children of the Kingdom. Is not that sufficient for thee? The Father asketh of thee the faith which is born of the Kingdom of Heaven.

Thou canst safely leave the evolving of the Eternal in the hands of Him who is the Eternal One.

The imagination of man s mind is unto Him extreme foolishness. All that thou hast known, all that thou hast believed, shall pass away before the wondrous surprise of immortal consciousness which awaiteth thee.

Empty thyselves; loosen thy hold upon the landmark that thou hast known. Cling to the Cross of Christ ONLY. The knowledge which thou hast has been of darkness; thou canst not conceive the Light which shall illumine thy Spiritual Being when thou hast entered more fully into the Mind of Christ.

THE Spirit of the Lord is not found in the byways of diverse creeds and earthly theories.

Knowledge is not happiness, and Science is but one kind of ignorance which mortals exchange for another kind of ignorance.

The Tree of Knowledge is not the Tree of Life. Philosophy, Science, the Wells of Wonder, and the Springs of Wisdom are of no avail to man, but shall be scorched into annihilation by the fiery blast of Spirit which hath illimitable domination over all.

Knowledge cannot design Me. Love painteth the inexpressible beauty of My Immortal Image with the colors which are likest unto the hues of Heaven.

Make not My Image according unto thine own construing, for I say unto thee: Thou art blind, thou art deaf, thou art slow of understanding.

The Lord is very present with thee. He holdeth His Court among the simple-hearted in His Kingdom of Heaven. The entrance is nigh unto him who accepteth the simplicity of the Lord.

Be as a child in the Land of Marvel: sweet unto God is the wonder of innocents,

Seek simplicity, and it shall be given unto you to find the Kingdom of Heaven.

GOD, the Father worketh many marvels, inexplicable to His children.

Give up that to which thou clingest; it holdeth thee hack from the Cross of God.

The Holy One hath His Pavilion among the Infinite Splendours; while Thou art very simple in His sight upon the earth, an infant as it were in the Spirit.

Thou canst not see, thou dost not know what are His Thoughts- Yet He asketh thee to come unto Him, to dwell with Him, to be unto Him as His child in the wondrous habitation of His Glorious Universe. The unspeakable glories that are His, the work of His own Creation shall be thine also; because He is thy Father.

The Spirit of God shall breathe through the Universe and thine eves shall behold the Incarnation of the Christ! Behold the Form of the Radiant One is present with thee!

Let thy words be simple and let thy speech be OF THE SPIRIT ONLY, that thou mayest build upon rock. Thou hast an Immortal Defender, His name is JESUS CHRIST. He hath simplified the mighty Truths of Eternity, and prepared the way for the innocent in Spirit. He knoweth His own, He carrieth the Lambs in His Bosom.

Divine Love lighteth, and glory thrilleth the hearts of those follow on in confidence and faith.

IMPORTANT

MOST of those receiving this Paper have been in this work now nearly four years. You have come a lone journey with us. although not all have accompanied us every step of the way. Some have loitered along the road, enticed perhaps by more alluring paths and wandering in them for awhile: or the travelling has been too strenuous or difficult and they could not keep up; but all such have tried to follow as best they could, receiving the teaching each month and striving to comprehend the hidden truths therein, hut failing to make the headway others have made who kept strictly upon the Impersonal Path, and who were determined to live the teachings.

The time has come when it is necessary to know all those who have traveled with us all the way, who have earnestly striven to prove the teachings, and who thereby have found the Kingdom and are now more or less living in and working from Its Consciousness.

You should all understand what we mean by having found the Kingdom. But we are going to be more explicit. and to ask you the following questions, which for a very important reason we wish everyone reading them to answer as fully and succinctly as possible, if you kindly will :

1. Are you sure you have found and are now being taught by the Comforter, your Christ Self? Explain why you are sure.

2. Are you looking to Him as your supreme Teacher and Authority, and depending on no one else? What comes to you as a result?

3. Are you able to command your human mind to "Be still, and know, I AM, God," and then know that you are the "I AM" Who commands, and that you and God are One? How can you prove this?

4. Are you sure you have found the Kingdom, and can you abide in it for any length of time? What does the Kingdom mean to you when you are in Its Consciousness?

5. Can you truly see Christ, the Higher Self, and Good or God, in everyone and in every thing and condition around you? What is this "seeing" doing to and for you?

6. Have you had any inner experiences—dreams or visions—in which you were with others robed in White? In them did you see the Lord Jesus? Describe such experiences and what they meant to you at the time.

7. Describe just what this Work means to you, what it has done for you, and what you deem it to be.

Because these are very vital questions concerning your sours welfare, we suggest that you ask your own Higher Self to you in the answering of them. Study each question carefully until you get its full meaning, and then wait for the inner leading before you write down your reply.

Write the answer to each question separately, numbering each as listed. and use a separate sheet of paper for these answers, dating the head of the sheet, and signing your name and address below. Try to get it to us as soon as you can.

Please do not expect an early acknowledgement of your response, for there be too many to answer in the coming month. Either a letter will follow before or with the October Paper, or in it there may be a further communication regarding this request.

From this you will see that have approached a new stage of the Work, and we wish everyone possible to be prepared for It

XII. IN HIS SERVICE"

PAPER 47, NOVEMBER, 1932

THIS Paper is going to be in the nature of a heart to heart talk with you.

We have journeyed together now for nearly four years, and we have gone far—those of you who have accompanied us all the way; and many wonderful things have been accomplished, especially by those who have earnestly striven to prove the truths unfolded to them.

By this time you will have realized that the questions in the September Paper were not asked to satisfy any personal interest in the disciples' understanding; but it was an opportunity given to enable each one to face him or herself and to learn just where each had arrived on this journey we are traveling.

Some of you found you had not gotten so very far and felt rather dismayed, especially when -you realized you could not answer positively and with definite knowing certain of the questions, which from the teachings received should have been learned and proven long ago. In answering these questions you surely also found what you have not yet attained, and what is still ahead. And so this article is to help you to realize it fully and to inspire you to more determined efforts to reach the final goal.

What is that goal? Some will say, the finding and abiding in the Kingdom.

But do you know what finding and abiding in the Kingdom means? The questions were designed to learn just that: also who were those who glimpsed and who were approaching the real goal—which is Divine Union, or the final uniting of your Higher and lower selves, or of your human consciousness with that of your Son of God Consciousness.

Let us try and show you the distinction. The finding of the kingdom is the heritage of every disciple of Christ. The. Christ Consciousness is the door the only way there, the only truth, and the only life that exists in the Kingdom.

Some of you have found the Kingdom. Some of you think you have found it. Some of you think you have found the Comforter. Yes, if you are allowing Him to teach you all things and to lead you unto all truth, and you know Him as God's Holy Spirit in you, your own Christ Self, truly a Son of God,—then you have indeed found the Comforter, and the final goal is near.

A disciple as you have been taught is one who is fob lowing the Christ, either Jesus Christ, our Beloved Master and Teacher; or the Christ within, the Comforter. These represent two different and distinct stages of unfoldment, as Jesus taught; the former leading into the latter, wherein the disciple has grown to the point where all outer teachers must leave him-—even including Jesus, so that the Holy Spirit, the Comforter, the Christ within, may forth unto His own, and henceforth be the sole Teacher and supreme Authority for the disciple.

It is The Christ within who then gradually disciple unto the finding. and abiding in the Kingdom. And as the consciousness unfolds and all outer attractions and Influences fade away into the nothingness from which they were created, and the Kingdom becomes the one and only life and the Great Reality, the last sense of self and of separateness disappears and the consciousness little by little, having found and now abiding in the Kingdom, takes on first the Power and later the Glory of the Christ, and knows Itself as I AM, a Divine Son of God, having finally returned to its Father's Home, His Consciousness, the real goal of the human soul.

To understand this clearly a full comprehension of the purpose of the soul's birth, nature, life expression and destiny   must be had, and these are definitely taught in Papers 9, 10 and 11 and subsequent articles. It is the soul in its long, long journey back to its Father's Home, its consciousness having strayed away many world periods before there was a planet earth, that is what is united again with its Father's, now a Son of God's Consciousness, and brings about the Great Consummation, the greatest that can be accomplished on this planet.

WE TELL you this now for a two-fold purpose—that you may have a confirmation of what some of you have glimpsed as a glorious possibility—yes, even for this life: and that it may spur you on to unrelenting efforts at co-operation with your Higher Self.

For remember, some of you are very old souls. All of you are old souls, and are here for a definite purpose closely related to Christ's second coming to Earth and His ushering in the New Dispensation. Therefore it behooves all who receive this Paper to think long and seriously over what has been stated and especially over what follows; for perhaps what we will show you is the most important thing that faces you in this life.

We wonder how many of you fully realize why you came into this Work: that it was no accident but that all your previous life, nay lives, were a preparation for It, and that you were definitively led to It to receive the final training and a clear understanding of WHY you are here in this present life, of WHO you are, and of WHAT you are a part.

You will note that the seventh and last question asks you to describe "just what this work means to you, what it has done for you, and what you deem it to be." It was from your answer to that question that we learned what you have really gained spiritually from your association with the Work. For only those who have a true understanding of what is this Work have any realization of Who they are and of What they are a part.

Do you grasp what that means? If not, it is because you have not yet glimpsed the real purpose of your own life, and why you are journeying with us, despite all the great truths have been sending you. The time is now here when we must make this so plain that those receiving this Paper will not fail to understand what is this Work and why they are a part of It – if they really are a part. And that each one will have to determine, after reading what follows.

We were lead recently to write the enclosed pamphlet explaining the inner purpose of the Impersonal Work, but we were not led to send out a copy of it, although it has been printed and ready for over eight weeks. We have simply waited until we were shown when and to whom to send it.

We are sending it herewith, and only at this time to you who have had all the Papers, because we consider you as one of us in your soul nature we are truly one with you, even though your human minds may not as yet realize it. Therefore you will understand and be glad to know all that is stated therein, for of course it is as much your concern as ours—you who are a part of this Work, as you will learn after carefully reading and prayerfully considering all its truths.

We are sending it to you then first to acquaint you with the inner nature of the Work, Its Spiritual importance, and what It is sent to accomplish in the world at this particular time; and then to spur you on to redoubled efforts to become an actual and integral part of It, to find your individual part and place in It; so that your heart's yearning will become so great that you will draw to you the means and opportunities for serving that the Master always provides for those who compel His attention.

Some of you of course have found this out already, and are wonderfully helping and serving, and much that is stated in the pamphlet does not apply to and is not intended for you, as is clearly shown therein.

In fact, this Paper has only to do with your Spiritual progress and concerns, the pamphlet but showing those who belong in the Work how intimately such progress and concerns are related to the needs, plans and possibilities of the Work Itself.

So with this preface we ask you to take up the pamphlet at this point and read it once slowly, before continuing this present article.

A GREAT many thoughts have come to us while reading and studying the several hundred answers to the questions received. We have learned from them who are the truly consecrated ones; and who those who are earnestly studying the Lessons but still allow the things of the world and self to come between and distract them from gaining the fulfillment of their souls' desires. In other words, the finding of the Kingdom is second, not first, with the latter.

Then there are those who clearly see in the Teachings great Spiritual Truths; who read each Paper two or three times, marvel over them, and wish they might gain and enjoy the blessings that undoubtedly await those more able to give the time and effort to their attainment. With these the finding of the Kingdom is third or fourth, many things crowding in between, and always causing a postponement of the effort they intend sometime to put upon proving the Truths.

Then we find there is a fourth group, who continue to receive the Teachings because of the stimulating effect it has on them for the time being—like going to church on Sundays. They do not want to miss any, love to read them, contribute to the Work; but make little if any real use of the Truths in their lives.

All this naturally makes us wonder how much further we should go in the sending of these priceless Truths to the second, third and fourth groups; for we clearly realize that enough, nay more than enough Truths have been given- —even in the first twenty Lessons—to enable any earnest, determined seeker long ago to have. found the Kingdom and to be abiding- and working in and from It now. We believe there IS no doubt of this in the mind of anyone reads And remember, in the first Paper it was stated that this Work was only for those who were making the finding of the Kingdom first and supreme ill their lives—not second or third or fourth.

We said at the beginning this would be a heart to heart talk with you. All of you have grown very dear to us, for during these four years we have received many letters telling of your problems, and into which we have entered with you, helping you to solve most of them; and naturally we are deeply concerned about your souls' welfare and want to see every one of you a conscious part of that Great Brotherhood of Christ to which you dedicated yourselves when coming into this Work.

Do you realize what we mean? Do you realize what it means to you to attain to a conscious knowing of your part in that Brotherhood? Do you realize what we are trying to do for you and to have you do?

Who are we who write these words to you? No, not the human personality through whom we write. He is but the consecrated instrument, the servant of the Brotherhood, and of himself is nothing. But having given himself to Christ, We of the Brotherhood, Who, remember, are all One in Christ, are able through him to reach you and show you these Divine Truths, in an effort to recall you to the purpose of your coming to Earth at this time, and of your contacting this Our Work.

For this is an effort of the Brotherhood to draw together all those who went into incarnation to be on Earth at this particular period; to awaken them to a realization of Who they are, and to uncover to their brain minds much of the Divine Truths they in their souls know, so they will be able to work for and with Us, when the Master calls them to definite service.

From this you will gather that most of you—the truly Christ consecrated ones—-are in your soul lives a part of the Brotherhood, and that tnc.se and unfold those faculties in you that will enable you to be fully conscious of Us and of your mission on Earth.

Those of you who have failed to recognize, from the Truths given, Who we are and what you are, and have deemed this Work but another effort on the part of some personality to give forth truths he had learned, and that they are similar, only more advanced, to the many other teachings you had already contacted, are the ones who on reading this now regret that they put so little study and effort on the Teachings—if what is stated herein has awakened them to a realization of its truth and of what they have missed.

On the other hand, if what is here said but confirms what some of you have felt deep within to be true, and your heart gladly responds and to make yourselves fully fit and ready for the Master's Call, We say to such strive daily to prove what has been shown you in the last few Papers, and particularly ASSUME now your identity as a Son of God, KNOW your Oneness with Us, ACT as a member of the Brotherhood, and BE a representative of Christ here on Earth, even as you are doing with Us now in Spirit.

In that attitude of mind and soul you link your outer consciousness with Ours and enable Us more easily to inspire and quicken in you the Christ powers that will enable you to throw off the sense of self and separation and to become wholly One with Us.

For of course we are very close to you, ever working to bring about that consummation, so you can work consciously with Us in the outer, even as the Inner.

Think what that means! You would be always then conscious of Us, conscious of your Christ powers, conscious of your home in the Kingdom, of your real life there, and that your life on Earth is but an illusion, a dream of your human mind, from which it is now awakened, so that it too now knows that You and You alone, and that it and its life and world are false dream-pictures it had been taught to believe were real, when the only reality IS what it now sees in You and Your life in the soul realm of consciousness.

That is what awaits all real disciples in the near future, and We give you this vision and promise to spur on your minds to more determined efforts—having now learned the great truths taught them—to surrender themselves utterly to the God in You. For they must by this time clearly realize that it is only their sense of separation from You that prevents Divine Union; and more than anything else We want to help them to let go of that sense—to yield all to God, so that He in and through You may accomplish what He has been preparing you for all of this life.

DO YOU want to ready when Christ Jesus comes, so you can meet Him "in the air," and can be with Him henceforth, ever working under His direction? Then, dear ones, this Work is to help you to make ready for that glad event.

Can you not see it? Cast off the illusions of the senses, all beliefs in separation and of mortality, and lift up your eyes and see Him in Spirit calling you and lovingly offering you a place in His Army of Light, among

His Warrior-Servers, Who are busy night and day carrying the Light of Christ to those still wandering in darkness.

The time is growing very short and the enemy forces are unbelievably active, using every possible means to lead those in whom they see any light into by-paths of error, deception and evil. On the other hand there are the vasts hosts of those whom they have exploited and kept in the darkness of ignorance, who if they could have brought to them the light of Truth, would eagerly follow that light to a full understanding of it. Therein are all possible workers on Earth needed—to save these lost sheep and bring them back into our beloved Master Shepherd's fold.

Another thing, We wish you to know that this is not in any sense an earthly organization with which you have aligned yourselves, but it is a heavenly organization, one that has existed from the beginning and is composed of the innumerable hosts of Angels, the General Assembly and the Church of the First Born, who are enrolled in heaven, and the Spirits of Just Men made Perfect;" and all working under "Jesus, the Mediator of the New Covenant," in complete co-operation with "God the Judge of all," and all "dwelling on Mount Zion, the heavenly Jerusalem, the City of the Living God," as spoken of by Paul in his Epistle to the Hebrews 12:22-24.

These are not mere fanciful terms describing an imaginary condition in a Utopian heaven, but are Paul's words telling of an actual organization of God's Officers and Warriors forming a great Army of Servers in the Spiritual Realms, whose sole aim and work is the redemption of humanity and the bringing of as many as possible into the Light of Christ, through the co-operation and assistance of Its members working among men on Earth.

Are you of Its members? Does your soul yearn to have you be a member? Surely by this time, from the many teachings received and all We have told you about this Army, you know; something within must tell you whether you are a member now, or that your soul intends that you be one as soon as your mortal self assents.

Erase from your mind all belief that in your mortal self you are anything; for you are a soul, a Spiritual being, and what your soul is, you are. And if your soul is a member of this Army, your human expression must fall in line and do the work of the Army.

Further rebellion on the part of the mortal self only brings suffering, mental and physical, and hardships of various kinds; until your mind realizes the soul's will and purpose and surrenders completely

Have you not had enough of suffering and hardship? Then why not yield to your soul now, and let it lead? The moment you truly surrender, the way will open wide, and all you need do will be to walk straight ahead, do what is before you to do, and everything will be made easy for you. Is not that better than the life of self you are now living?

THIS has indeed been a heart to heart talk, and now we have come to the place where We must ask you what is your wish and purpose as to this Work. Are We to send you more Lessons, when you have not really learned many that you already have? Or should We cease for awhile, until you get caught up and prove to Us you are ready for more?

Or shall We give you some definite work to do, and by the evidence you furnish of your ability to do that work well, will We know what to send you next?

From this you can see We are deeply concerned about your Spiritual needs, and that We want to help you to come quickly into that consciousness where you can be of the greatest possible value and assistance to the Brotherhood. Not that We do not know that your own Higher Selves know best what you need and will always provide just the help and guidance necessary; but as We of the Brotherhood are One in Christ with your Higher Selves, We through Our agent in the outer are helping Them do bring your human minds into a realization of the necessity of earnest and steadfast consecration to the Work from this time on—those of you whose souls are really a part of It and of the Brotherhood.

One thing more. We have noticed in the past that those who have grown the fastest and made the greatest progress Spiritually are those who have kept in close touch with the Center, writing often and of the things dearest to their hearts, thus proving their deep interest in the Work and of their desire to fit themselves for the Master s service.

Because of this fact, we are wondering if it were not best in the future to devote our time and efforts only with such truly in earnest ones. Not that we seek to take on the additional task of the increased correspondence such help will entail by thus inviting it, but that if it will aid those disciples who are determined speedily to reach the goal, no labor on the part of any or all members of the Brotherhood will be too great to bring about that result. For the more consecrated conscious Brothers We, have working in the outer, the more sure and speedy will be Our victory over the forces of darkness.

In conclusion We now ask you to think over most carefully all of the above, reading it again and again, until all of its real meaning becomes clear in your consciousness. These four years we have journeyed together have been frought with deep and vital consequences to your souls and these consequences have been reflected in your outer lives. Do you wish to go on the conclusion of what your souls intend? If so, are you willing and ready do your part?

Then write us your ideas, your intention, your wishes. For upon them will be based the future policy of this outer phase of the Master's Work.

REGARDING the answers to the questions, they are being gone over as fast as possible, and are being

graded into the four groups mentioned. Not all answers are in, and We are going to assume that those who have not responded, or who do not respond after receiving this Paper, are not sufficiently interested and therefore do not belong with us. They will receive no more Papers or communications. Your reply to the above will be attached to your answer to the questions and will help Us to place you with regard to the possible work We may call upon you to do in the Master's Service.

NO.

Do you realize what a wonderful power and significance is hidden ill this little word ' 'No?'

Very few, even so-called Truth students, have had their attention called to this mighty little word, and for the good reason that they have not yet unfolded to the point spiritually and mentally where they can comprehend and use its power.

There are those among you, however, who are ready, so in this short article we will open up the subject, preparing you for a more elaborate treatise to be brought out in booklet form, and to which this will serve in the nature of an Introduction.

There are few that are able properly to say, "No," and say it. Why? Because they do not definitively and positively know if they mean ' 'No" when they say it. Think, and see if this is not true.

Of course, if you are one of those "positive" individuals who always know your own mind, or think you do, you may say "No" often, and create the impression of speaking with knowledge and authority. But even with such the real power and meaning of "No" may not be comprehended.

Can you conceive of an individual who, when a wrong thought or belief his body, his life, his affairs, about another person comes to his mind, can say, "No' with such power that such thought or belief instantly disappears from his consciousness, and it no longer exists to him?

Do you grasp what we mean? Think this over for a moment, before you continue reading.

We mean that when the true power of speaking the word "No" is gained or unfolded in you, not only does the wrong thought or belief disappear from your consciousness, but if it was in manifestation as a physical fact, condition or an appearance of any kind deemed to be real— it will actually and immediately dissolve and appear no more.

Do you think that possible? It is not only possible but it can be proven by anyone who can clearly see—that all outer manifestations are but creations of the mortal separate mind, and if they are not wholly good, beautiful and perfect even as God sees them, they are counter-fits and imperfect pictures of the real things, conditions or beings that exist in the Kingdom. It can be proven by simply seeing instead the true image as it exists in the Kingdom, and positively and with all the power and feeling of your soul saying

"No," to any false picture, there by wiping it completely out of consciousness. As surely as it is thus wiped out of consciousness it is wiped out of physical existence

To give an illustration of how this truth works, we will tell of an incident published in a Truth Magazine a number of years ago that made so powerful an impression upon the writer that it has always remained vivid in his mind. He has seen similar proofs in minor ways many times since in his own and others' experience.

A Truth Practitioner was visited one day by a woman whose face was horribly distorted by an enormous tumor. The moment the Practitioner saw the face the horror of it so stirred her soul that it roused all the conviction of Truth in her to the surface, and with holy indignation and voice filled with the divine power stirring her, she said :

'No! You are abominable lie! There is no truth or reality in you; for you do not exist in God's Mind. Begone, and free this soul for God's true expression and use!

She then closed her eyes, and saw the God expression in that soul, and praised and thanked GOD that His Truth and Perfection exist as the One and Only Reality.

When she opened her eyes, she was not surprised --because of the intensity of her feelings and vision—to see half the tumor gone and it actually disintegrating and being absorbed inwardly before her eyes. In a short time it was almost gone: and in a few days the face showed few signs of its former disfigurement.

When you can consciously know and experience this power in you and arouse it at need, can you not realize the mighty force you have at your command' And when you can concentrate it at will in this little word "No ' you can drive out of your consciousness, your nature, your life undesirable factor, quality, state or condition, and see in Its place the perfect state existing God Mind, and actually see it all change before your eyes, even as did the Practitioner in the. experience described.

Therefore, beloved, know that this power is yours as a Son of God, that you are a Spiritual Being having dominion over the flesh and over all physical or outer states and conditions.

Study carefully the way the Practitioner Destroyed and dematerialized the lie on the face of the woman, who was carrying it about in her consciousness until it outmanifested in that horrible tumor.

Study the Practitioner's intense feelings and how she utilized them by pouring them into those powerful Words of Truth, using the wedge-word "No" to break down the mental opposition of the woman. Realize that these intense feelings are the mighty forces of Spirit ever ready to come forth at will for the accomplishing of any need in your life or in the life of another. Study and learn from it all how to control, direct and utilize these forces, for herein is disclosed to you a very wonderful and much needed Truth.

As said before, this is but a taste of what is possible in The conscious and true use of The word "No." We have In press a booklet of that title, by A. Lura Douglas, that should be ready for delivery in thirty days. a book on the Pyramid, giving its symbolic meaning and showing that there is a very wonderful analogy in its various passages, anterooms and chambers to the growth and development of a man's soul and the unfoldment of his Spiritual powers. You will be very agreeably surprised and greatly profited by studying and proving the truths of this little book.

XIII. AN EASTER MESSAGE

PAPER No. 52, APRIL, 1933

ALL WHO have taken seriously what has been said in the heart to heart talks we have had the last four months — and we earnestly hope all have so taken it — must realize that we have been trying to prepare every member of *The Impersonal Work* for something most important, and that we have been so strongly impressing the necessity of finding and abiding in the Christ Consciousness for a very definite purpose.

We have indicated this almost from the beginning, but now the time has come when the need has grown so great that we shall make one more appeal — to those who have followed with us and have not yet found and entered It, to lay aside everything now for a supreme effort to find the Kingdom, which of course means the Christ Consciousness; and in very truth to make that effort FIRST, above every other thing else in life.

Remember, when coming into this Work, you came allowing us to assume that you were responding to the call given and were *then* making the finding of the Kingdom FIRST. But can you face your Higher Self, and our Great Leader, Christ Jesus, and say it has actually been *first* during all these past four years?

Do you realize what that means? And can you now see why you have not found the

Kingdom? And why others *have* found it? For it has been FIRST — not second or third — to everyone who has found the Kingdom. Yes, it must be the one and only desire of the heart — the only thing for which you are now living. For surely you have caught at least a glimpse of why you are here; of what life here has meant, and the purpose of it — that you are but preparing your human instrument for something that is the sole reason for your being in physical expression?

Whether your human mind has deemed that glimpse of any significance before this, matters not. NOW, we make this further appeal to you to wake up — you who are still lagging behind because of other matters that are allowed to interfere.

Are there any other things of more importance than what we have asked? If you do not believe us, then neither do you believe our beloved Master, Who said, *"Seek ye FIRST the Kingdom of God and His Righteousness — AND ALL THINGS ELSE WILL BE ADDED."*

Can we offer you any more than He thus promised? Yet you dally, and think, fret and worry about all those petty, futile things in the outer, that are fast slipping from your grasp, being taken from you by your Higher Self, so that there will be nothing more to hinder your coming within into the Kingdom of His Consciousness — causing you to surrender every outer desire, and to center all your forces upon finding and abiding in Him.

Of course we have said this over and over again many times, in different words and in various ways. And why think you we have said it and have been so persistent? We and your Brothers of the Kingdom are trying to wake you up and to remind you why you are here in incarnation and of the work that lies ahead and which you come here expressly to do.

As we said above, the time is here when you must make a supreme effort to regain your True Consciousness, and thus prepare your human expression for active service. The Call has come for *conscious* workers. Are you one? If not, why not? Because you have not yet found your Divine Self within — despite all the teaching, helps and opportunities given you the past four years — all due to your not making the effort you knew you should make.

But that is past. NOW is the accepted time. And if you will make that supreme effort today and every hour hereafter, actually making the gaining of the Christ Consciousness FIRST, it will be granted you.

And to that end we are offering you the following chance to earn what is already yours, waiting for you to claim it.

AN EASTER MESSAGE

WE HAVE arrived at another Easter Season, when all nature is preparing to burst forth into a renewed and beautiful expression of the Life within, which through its myriad forms thus pictures to the minds of men what lies within the soul of Nature.

Likewise in man, the highest and most perfect form in which Life dwells, is It trying to come forth and express to man's mind the beauty and perfection of what lies deep within *his* nature—a part of the great Cosmic Nature.

At each Easter Season, whether he is aware of it or not, does man advance one stage nearer to that beauty and perfection, until finally he reaches Spiritual maturity; when he recognizes his part in the All, gives himself to the All, and ever afterward seeks to co-operate with and let the beauty and perfection of the Life within come forth and express in glorious harmony with the Life in nature everywhere about him, in the outer as well as in the inner world.

And by this same token are there many souls who reach maturity during each Harvest Season, and who the following Spring at Easter time come to their blossoming stage, and are there brought into conscious realization of their Divine Estate, in the soul realm.

This Life within man and within all nature is the Life of our Father God and is called the Christ Life, because it expresses through the Life of His Son, the Christ, Who represents the Father and is our Lord God on planet Earth. But as was said before, not until that Life has built a perfect form in man, and the outer consciousness is unfolded to where it can co-operate fully with the Christ Life within, is that form matured and ripened; and so at each Easter Season, for all souls who have reached that stage, a great celebration is held in the soul realm to rejoice over the return of these sons of God again to their Father's Home, and at the same time to celebrate the rebirth of the Christ in them.

For this reason have we been trying to prepare you for that return, by giving you a foretaste of it in the joy of working with your brothers in small groups in the outer. We have tried to have you realize that in group work alone can you come into a consciousness of that great Inner Group of which your souls are a part. For somehow, when in the company of kindred souls, all meeting in His Name and seeking to fit and make themselves worthy for His Service, does such realization come, sooner or later; especially when those in the group have risen above personality and have learned to see through the eyes of Love and to know with their Christ understanding the real reason for their thus coming together.

Only through group consciousness is the Christ Consciousness attained, and only through the Christ Consciousness is the Consciousness of the Great Christ Brotherhood attained. Group consciousness may have been attained in a previous life, and the other Consciousness is to be earned and gained in this life. Likewise, the Christ Consciousness may have been attained in a former life, and the Consciousness of the Brotherhood must be earned and acquired in this life. But each and all are gained *only through an intense yearning to serve.* Such yearning will eventually carry you to the highest.

At this Easter Season a great gathering of Christ Conscious souls will meet together as usual at Jerusalem in the soul realm. Among them will be many who are incarnated in the flesh, doing their part in keeping moving the complicated machinery of the outer world.

Many of those present will be Christ Conscious in the outer as well as in their soul consciousness, and at the coming celebration a considerable number of those who have attained to such consciousness the past year will be welcomed into the Great Brotherhood. They from then on will work consciously with their Brothers in the outer world to bring as many more as possible into the Light of the Christ Consciousness.

Through the efforts of all these workers the band of outer conscious members will soon grow to vast proportions, all working for the Christ Cause; each succeeding Easter seeing larger and ever larger numbers of new members initiated into the Group on the inner plane. But no matter how powerful and far-reaching the Work may become in the outer, none will be admitted to the band of workers until they have first become truly conscious of the Christ within and are waiting upon and serving Him there. In such manner will the Work be kept pure and unpolluted until the actual coming of God's Kingdom on Earth, through the efforts of these selfless ones, who will be truly doing the work of the Kingdom even while here in the outer. We wish all to note the distinction between being Christ Conscious, and being Conscious of the Christ *within;* also between the followers of Jesus Christ and those Who are following and serving Divine Teachers or Masters of other Faiths.

Try to realize that one who is conscious as Jesus was of His Oneness with the Father, is not the same as one who is waiting upon and serving the Christ *within* for the latter is still separate from Him and has not yet come into His Consciousness. His Consciousness, however, awaits all those who *prove* their love for and trust in Him as the Holy Spirit of their Loving Father, God.

On the other hand, those who are serving and waiting upon other Holy Ones or inner Masters or Teachers, are being taught and prepared to find and know God's Holy Spirit *within themselves*: while all those who love and are following the teachings of Jesus, are likewise growing and unfolding to the stage where they can become aware of Christ, the Comforter within, instead of just loving and venerating Him Who lived and taught these great truths nineteen hundred years ago.

This would mean that those who are following other Faiths and other Teachers, no matter how beautiful their teachings or how wonderful the powers of such Teachers, unless these Teachers always point to and help their followers to find God's Holy Spirit within themselves, they are not being consciously guided by that Spirit and are therefore still in the consciousness of self and of separation.

All men, no matter what their religion or faith, no matter what Divine Teacher or Master they are loving and following, eventually will unfold in consciousness to where Divine Love, God's Holy Spirit, the Comforter, will come forth and rule in their minds and hearts, will then live His Life, do His Will, and be their one and only Self.

When the Comforter comes to a man, as Jesus promised, He will teach him all things and lead him unto all truth; which means will lead him straight to the Kingdom of God's Consciousness, and he will then be concerned only about doing his Father's will on earth even as in Heaven.

For such, the Kingdom is not only a reality in the inner realm, but it will have become a reality in the outer; for in doing the work of the Kingdom they are thus inevitably and surely bringing the Kingdom down upon the Earth. Think on this, until you see how true it must be.

WE TELL you all this for one purpose only — to show you what awaits your placing all of self upon the altar to be burned, giving yourself as a living sacrifice to the Father, that He may accept and endue you with the power to serve selflessly and to make your human self into a perfect instrument for Christ and the Brotherhood's use.

This must be the one desire of your heart from now on — if you are to be a conscious participator in the Easter Services and conscious of your membership in the Great Christ Brotherhood. And above all must this desire be untainted by a personal longing so to participate with or to be conscious of your Brothers in Spirit. You must give up all desire for such pleasures, for they are of the self, and will only hold you back from the real attainment that your soul intends for you.

Therefore, make careful analysis of your desires, both open and secret, and see that nothing is reserved and the surrender is complete. Then place all upon the altar, and abide serenely in the silence of your soul, allowing the Divine One there to take full charge and to lead henceforth.

Above all things, dear ones, our desire is for you to reach the goal this Easter time. For that, for which you have been so long preparing your human instruments, awaits, and we would that you may participate in it.

What we have stated above we have made as strong as we could, to impress upon you its vital importance. Of course none of it applies to those who *know* they have already come into their Christ Consciousness and are now more or less thinking, speaking and acting from it.

If any experiences have come since answering the questions in Paper 45, that you have not told us, but which convince you that you have made the grade, we earnestly urge that you write us of them at once. We are preparing for some definite work and every Christ Conscious worker that is available will be needed in it. We hope that you can write us that you are now ready for Inner Service.

XIV. THE GRACE OF GOD

PAPER No. 63, MARCH, 1934

WE WISH to talk in this Paper of Grace, that word often used in the scriptures, but which very few understand in its full significance. Many quotations could be given, but we have chosen a few that we will consider, trying to show their true meaning.

Paul tries to tell us in his Epistle to the Romans, 11:2-8, what constitutes God's Grace:

God hath not cast away his people which he foreknew. Wot ye not what the scripture saith of Elias? How he maketh intercession to God against Israel, saying,

Lord, they have killed thy prophets, and digged down thine altars; and I am left alone, and they seek my life.

But what sayeth the answer of God unto him? "I have reserved to myself seven thousand men, who have not bowed the knee to the image of Ba-al."

Even so then at this present time also there is a remnant according to the election of grace.

And if by grace, then is it no more from works; otherwise grace is no more grace.

What then? Israel hath not obtained what he seeketh; but the *Chosen* obtained it, and the rest were blinded;—

As it is written, "God hath given them the spirit of slumber, eyes that should not see, and ears that should not hear," even till this very day.

There can be no question that there is a remnant of the elect or chosen ones of Israel in the world today, who have not bowed the knee to the image of Ba-al. These have *found favour* in God's sight.

Then if they have found favour (and the translation from the original Greek Text uses the word favour instead of grace), it is no more a case of striving and working to obtain it; the Grace of God is with them — *is theirs to use,* and there must be the continual outpouring of His Spirit through them, empowering them to do all things in His Name.

But they must *know* this *in their outer minds,* and must require their minds to accept of this truth, and with it the Grace of God that awaits.

We today are as Paul and the Apostles exhorting you, the children of Israel, God's chosen people, to awaken to your divine birthright. For you would not be reading these words if they were not meant for you as chosen ones. Therefore, read also Paul's other words in this 11th chapter of Romans and continue into the 12th chapter, and learn how surely he is speaking to you today as much as he was to the Israelites of his day, in his desire to bring all the chosen ones to the blessings that await. And remember that the real Israelites, God's chosen people, are all those who have found Him in their hearts, have accepted Jesus Christ and His Teachings as *God's Word* speaking direct from out their hearts, and who are following Him only.

Know that all that has gone before was given you by the Grace of *God in you*; all these teachings, all these great truths were but to prepare you for the awakening to the realization of His Grace, ever waiting to come forth and work His power in and through you.

Listen to the translation from the original Greek Text of Paul's words in the 25th to the 27th verses:

For Brethren, that ye may not be conceited with yourselves, I wish you not to be ignorant of this secret, that hardness in some measure (trials and testings) has happened to Israel (those God has called to His Service), till the fullness of the Gentiles may come in (till the fullness of the folly of the rulers of this world has become known).

And then shall all Israel be saved, as it has been written, "The Deliverer shall come out of Zion, and shall turn away ungodliness from Jacob (the Holy Spirit, the Comforter, will come with His Grace and shall drive out all darkness, flooding the mind with light, enabling the chosen ones (Israel) to know God's will, love and purpose in their fullness)."

And "This is the Covenant with them from Me, *when I shall take away their sins.*"

Surely it is a case of earning it, of growing to it, of becoming ready. All nature proves that nothing can come to its fruitage until its time. But you may say, if such is the case, how can we *earn* it if it is only a matter of growth?

In reply we will ask, *what* is growing, and who—what is growing it?

Are not You, a Son of God, growing and making perfect Your instrument, Your human personality, so that You can take charge and use it perfectly in the Father's Service? You are doing this to Your instrument, even as the Father, through Jesus Christ, is doing it to humanity. Are You not guiding, teaching, helping and in every way possible bringing to Your human mind a knowledge of its Oneness with You and with God, so that there may be nothing left in its consciousness to hinder Your perfect expression?

Shall we tell how You are doing this? First, through all previous experiences You prepared Your mind for this journey to the Kingdom you are taking with us. Then You brought to the mind's attention the Impersonal Teachings, that it might learn as fast as it was able just what is the mind, what is self, what is the soul, what is the Spirit, and what is *You*, and its relation to each; then how to let go of self, its concerns, its desires, its emotions, and all the things that are separating it in consciousness from You and God.

NOW ALLOW US to point out to your mind the way this was done. Try to grasp what follows, so that once and for always it will understand clearly the great value of the Impersonal Teachings.

In every Paper there were given many deep and important truths. Of these truths, each one was intended to be studied and stayed with until all of its inner meaning was uncovered and made a part of the consciousness — *before going on to the next.* We know that very few did this, for many report that they are going back to the beginning again and again, and each time find many truths they failed to discover before.

Let us consider what would have happened had you made your mind do what was intended, in the light of your past actual experience.

When a truth is stayed with and made a part of the consciousness — and by that is meant, when that truth is automatically used and acted upon, you find yourself freed from something that has been limiting you or holding you back. When a truth that is presented is thus faced until its hidden power is liberated, you find you have risen above some weakness, quality or condition that was preventing your highest expression. Each truth thus mastered brought about an expansion of consciousness that actually lifted you *above* what you were before.

Then think what would have happened had your mind faced each truth in each Paper until its power was built into the consciousness! It would have been like feeling something substantial, strong and permanent forming underneath, gradually lifting you above the old states of mind and freeing you from their fallacies and illusions and all their hindering influences, into a realm where you were seeing with ever clearer understanding those forces of self that so long had held you down to earth and its harsh bondage.

Each truth, in fact, was a brick that was intended to be laid in the structure that was to form your Spiritual Understanding. These bricks had to be laid in the order given, or the structure would not be sound and permanent; for they would fit well only in their proper places. In fact, each lesson in each Paper was prepared to lift the mind in consciousness One stage higher; so of course unless that stage had been truly reached and you were established thereon through your mastering each truth in a lesson, it would be impossible to stay there — any truth not thoroughly understood would weaken the support, and you would necessarily have to go back and build more surely and substantially.

This is proven by what you yourself have found, as stated above, Yes, you have all grown, but how substantially? Do you truly understand and are able to use in your daily life all the truths in the Papers? If not, you can now see why.

You have only to look back at the states of mind you were in one year, two years, five years ago, and see how much you have grown in spite of this; showing that even a few truths mastered will free and lift you out of the old consciousness and above conditions that hampered in the past. But now you can also see what might have been, had you made yourself study and stay with each truth given you during the last five years!

Why, dear ones, had you done this, you would now be One with Christ, your Divine Self; and would be using all the powers of God, your Father in Heaven, even as Jesus was using them when on earth!

Can you deny this? Can you now see why we have been so insistent on your doing what was so often urged? Not one thing was urged that would not help lift you above those weaknesses, qualities and limitations of self that were holding you down to their level and preventing your being where all might be now — in the Kingdom, and your serving as conscious Members of the Great Brotherhood of Christ.

In your souls you know this. Can we make it any stronger?

Of course this is meant only for those who feel that they are not getting as much from the lessons as they should, and to point them to what is necessary — if they wish to accompany us all the way. It may help all of our members to see more clearly the only right way to study these precious truths so that the mind and soul can grow and unfold consciously under the direction of the Loving One within.

May the Grace of the Lord Jesus Christ, and the Love of God, and the Communion of the Holy Spirit, be with you all. Amen.

HIS GRACE IS SUFFICIENT

WE WERE discussing the subject of Grace with some of our dear ones the past month, when one of them later, while meditating on its deep meaning, received the following message. Note how Grace is the last gift bestowed by God, and that with it comes a *sure knowledge,* the spiritualizing of what before was faith and belief.

DEAR Brother:

May the peace, the Love and the Grace of Christ Jesus be thy heritage and that of thy Brethren, who also are my Brethren.

Let this message be known to thee: Thou seekest Love and Wisdom and Peace. Let this be thy assurance; that God is all these, and more. But God does not give of Himself to them that strongly desire Him, though

He is a jewel beyond price and greatly to be desired; neither can this gift be earned by them that seek to possess it solely for themselves.

Art thou so blind that thou canst not see it is the trophy *given* to them that win the race; that fight the good fight against selfishness? What is selfishness? It is the desire that man gain for himself, even to bless others, any gift that adds one inch to his stature.

Be not misled, dear brother; God seeks out the one who can blot out the thought of self so utterly that he ceases to exist himself. Dost thou prate of humility, of love, of anything of God, and thinkest thou deniest self? Then thou art a liar. When self is truly selfless, then art thou unable to talk of humility, of mercy of love; for being wholly God — or Spiritual — it doth then speak for itself.

When thou canst lose thyself in God — knowing without limitation that thou art nothing, — *then*, and not until then, art thou abiding in Love or in the Great Heart of God.

How canst thou, being of flesh, give thyself utterly to God, Who is Spirit, and yet remain flesh? Cease thy strivings to attain Spiritual gifts — to heal, to demonstrate. When thou art truly learned, then thou dost know with sureness that God *is all there is,* and there is nothing beside Him. In this manner doth Grace come — then is it not possible for thee to make *any* claims; for His Grace is sufficient.

In thy heart is a question, — What is Grace? Know ye that Grace is the last gift bestowed upon thee, and comes with the *sure knowledge* that God, and God alone, worketh all things, and that thou canst not alter by a hair anything that God is; that God, being unseen, worketh in secret. And what canst thou do, Oh Child of man, but realize that that which hath not depth, nor breadth, and therefore is not to be measured, is God.

Learn this lesson; it is necessary before thou canst taste of the hidden Manna, which is truly the Bread of Life. Peace.

INNER EXPERIENCES

WE ARE happy to state that our last talk caused our friends to read and study more carefully the letter from the dear soul in the 61st Paper, and more than a few have written of the illumination and blessing that resulted therefrom.

But we also find there are still some who think it not worthwhile, feeling either they can get nothing from its seemingly foolish or childish statements, or that they understand all they care to know of what she "is trying to say."

In answer to such we invite them to go with us in consciousness with our dear sister through her experiences while we explain the spiritual significance of the wonderous things she described. They may ask how we know that she understands them as we do?

In Spirit there is only one language, and that is understood by all who are able to retire into the consciousness of their Christ Selves and allow the Spirit to unfold its meaning — which we have been trying to aid you who read these words to do for many months past.

But before giving you our spiritual interpretation, we are going to quote from some of the letters received, that you may know their views and what some think of such experiences. In the first one that follows only part is given of what was received during meditation — there not being enough space for all of it.

OH GOD, when you call me by name, what do you call me?

"A....., My dear A..... . You are My obedient A..... You seek only to do My will. Presently we shall be One indeed, with no other consciousness but Mine. You *are* My beloved child in whom I am well pleased. Let the Joy of My Life flow through every cell of your body, which is My body. See My body as pure Spirit, perfect and whole. I have taken your cross from you and lifted you up many times. Let Me always carry the burden of your cross. In My Consciousness there are no burdens — just Joy and Bliss ineffable. Glory in My Cross, A..... ; We can save the world when you cheerfully bear the Cross of Christ, that all may look up and see its Glory shining."

"Oh God, my Father, hold my hands. Let them be Thy hands, that I may do Thy work in the world."

"Yes, My child. Be still and know that I do all things. I use your hands, your heart, your mind, that My good may manifest always."

"Father God, earnestly I study Thy great Book of Truth, Thy Book of Remembrance."

"A..... , remember who thou art, a son of the Living God. Remember you are His outer expression. Hold your head high, yet know humbleness of spirit."

"I thank Thee, Father, for Thy great heart of matchless Love that is open to me and to all Thy children."

"Enter, My child, at the Straight Gate."

"Father, I vision that Gate, that no man can shut. I enter and I am alive for evermore, full of Peace that passeth understanding. I am covered there by the garment of Thy Love, shielded, protected and divinely guarded. Father I thank Thee. Because of Thy great Love, I have passed in safety over dark seas of doubt and despair. Thy wings bear me aloft. Light shines in my being. I enter and abide in the Holy of Holies." " 'Sun of my soul, Thou Saviour dear. It is not night when Thou art near.' "

"I know Thee as God, the Son, and the Holy Spirit — all One in me, Thy instrument. I serve Thee joyfully. I listen and let Thy Word speak through my mouth. Even my mouth is not mine but Thine. Thou use it only, dear God."

"THE 61st Paper, is a marvelous number when one can enter the proper consciousness to understand it. The first time I read the lesson with the mind only, and did not see so much in it, but after entering the Spiritual consciousness and meditating upon the symbols used, I found them very wonderful. Some of them are not unlike my own experiences. For instance, on Sunday night I entered meditation with the earnest desire for further light for this New Year of 1934, and almost immediately found myself enveloped in a white mist, the Christ right by me; and for a moment I was overwhelmed with joy. Then I seemed to be withdrawn within Him, could see my body, but it appeared empty; and Oh the happiness of that conscious moment when I realized that I, in my Higher Self, *was* the Christ, and there was no longer a lower self — just the instrument through which the Christ worked. 'Oh', I declared, 'I *am*, I *am*, I *am!*' Then again when I was in the body, I was still in His Consciousness. And how different everything seemed. There nothing mattered — so long as I could remain in that loving hallowed place."

"I NOW think I should have written this before, since reading the points on the Inner Meaning in that wonderful Paper, No. 62; so that you might be reassured that some of the humbler students found the inner meaning of that beloved soul whose message came so purely through her halting words. 'I was there on my knees — with His feet, *inside* His garment,' came from an experience so deep and holy that I am thankful to be allowed a contact with one at once so childlike and so high."

"THE experiences of others are great helps, and I have received much Light from those of our dear illumined one. We all know these things intellectually; but only when we contact one who has *experienced* these truths do they become real to us.

"It is so marvelous consciously to *feel* these great truths; the mind's consciousness being drawn into the Christ Consciousness so gently and lovingly (these surges of life become more and more frequent as one learns to search out their inner meaning), one sincere thought of God immediately creates this inner wave of silent power that opens the understanding so that it all stands forth a living reality."

THE INTERPRETATION

NOW FOR our interpretation of some of the more interesting and illuminating symbols. Try to realize that through her *feeling* the great Love for God and the Lord Jesus, which is really God's Love pouring out of her heart, her mind pictures this Love as God or Jesus — as Their very *Presence,* and that everything she experienced is but her *feelings* thus out-pictured.

Study our meaning until you get it, and try to prove it by carefully watching the pictures that form in your mind when you feel intensely any emotion — no matter what. Those of you who love God very dearly will discover, whenever you pray to Him or to Christ, that unconsciously you hold some kind of a picture of Them in your mind. Well, a strongly psychic type of mind will clearly see that picture, while the mental type will take no note of it, unless consciously watching for it, as we have suggested.

For instance, when she asked God to use His power for her, and "He was looking at me so Wonderfully, His eyes so full of love," that Love she actually *felt so strongly* that she pictured It as being God.

When He "called her by name," it was but her response to Love's inner call; and for three days she was submerged in that Love. What passed during that period she tries to describe, as her mind reasons or pictures it out for her.

Have you ever asked questions of the Loving One within, and received similar loving replies? We hope you all have, and that you now understand how some of the replies came.

When it "came" to her that *"I, God, alone Am,"* and the shepherd burned the big Cross on her bosom while God held her arms, it was but her yielding herself to this Great Love, allowing It to hold and restrain her human self while Love's Cross was burned on her heart so that she could feel It always — could feel *It only,* and know "It alone Is" — the guiding influence of her life.

In her deep meditation upon this she tells how she humbly prayed, and on opening her eyes saw *Jesus* on her Cross. Jesus only pictured to her, her crucified self; and of course as she looked on self thus, it was lifted up for her to see more clearly — see that it was the Christ of her on the Cross stretching out His arms to her to draw her to Him. Stop here until it all unfolds to you and you get the picture, its glorious meaning, and that of the words in the following paragraph in the Paper.

Now try to imagine yourself going inward through the Cross, The Cross represents the sacrifice or giving up of self, which when really done enables you to go inward in consciousness toward a great Light. But Love was with her, enfolding her in His arms, even as she described; and it must have been "a wonderful time." When she wrote her name on His chest, it was but her simple childlike response to His Love. And when He wrote His Name in her right hand, it was Love's natural response to such yielding of self — the transferring of Love's Power to her, *to use* — in His Name.

It was and is "very wonderful to be led by (Love) Jesus, and a great joy to be with Him." And when Love opens wide and allows you to enter His Consciousness, you do indeed find there a "big book" of knowledge and the six lights or sacred centers of the soul are lit, making us wish never to leave this Consciousness until all of its precious knowledge is unfolded to us.

So there she abode for some time, feeling the great reverence she describes, going down on her knees in prayer; when an Angel with Jesus in a new white robe appeared to her, symbolizing the glorification of Love or God's Holy Spirit in her consciousness, as she had never seen or felt it before; which naturally lighted the seventh, or holiest center, and Love wholly reigned, taking the place of self entirely. Then Love descends and covers her (enfolds her soul) completely, and she is filled with His Understanding, and she dwells there many days.

In that great Love and her desire never to leave It, she turns to God praying if Love's Cross has brought her all this joy that It never leave her; when, because of her unselfishness and true worship of Him, God's grace caused the Cross to shine *through* her, appearing on her back as well as in front of her, thus giving her all of Its Light; so that she could walk outward towards God in humanity, as well as inward toward Him in Spirit. And she attempts to describe what she saw as she walked inward. See if you can get what she means, what was meant by the devil appearing, and by her being victorious over him.

By this time, if you have followed understandingly with us every step of the way, what follows will not seem so preposterous — a door opening in Jesus' leg, her going through it and up a stairway and stopping before every Holy Place, and coming at last to the open door of His Heart, where Jesus was standing waiting to welcome her. For you will realize it was but her naive way of picturing how in her Christ Understanding the way opened permitting her to rise higher (or go further inward) in consciousness, until she found herself before the Holy Places, on her way to the Holy of Holies, the Secret Place of the Most High, where Divine Love waited to lead her.

In this Secret Place it is indeed dark, for she is stripped of every mortal sense and she has to make her way alone (for there for awhile even Love leaves her) into that Realm of Glory. She must earn it by fearlessly conquering every force, known and hidden, still left in her nature.

Finally she reaches the goal, the very center of her being, where God awaits, there finding Jesus and God are One, and that it was Their Love that was leading, inspiring, supporting and strengthening her all the way.

THIS gives you but a glimpse of what you might have got, had you stayed with each symbol when first read until Spirit unfolded its meaning for you. This meaning would have been "spiritual," the above being mere words and meaning but little unless you get in a consciousness that understands them, even as you must get in a deeper consciousness before Spirit can give you direct any symbol's meaning.

We are trying to impress upon all who heretofore have not had the patience to stay with a truth until they have wooed from Spirit its blessing, that they will never get anywhere spiritually, or in the acquirement of the very faculties and powers they seek, until they make themselves do what we have shown. Such is the only way to meditate properly, — to concentrate upon a truth, a symbol, or any abstruse statement, until you have compelled it to give up its meaning. In other words you must keep boring into consciousness until it opens up and discloses to you what you seek.

Think you this is impossible? It may have been so to you — because of your lack of patience or of faith in the Spirit in you. But we say to you, it is the only way to get acquainted with Spirit, to woo It, to get It to serve, teach and bless you.

Dear friend, It is always waiting to do this; but It reserves Its secrets arid Its blessings only for those who seek and want them more than anything else in life — and then only for use in the Father's service. It has no use for the weak, the mentally lazy, or the skeptical; for impatience, vacillation, or lack or persistence and courage. But It loves, and works with those who have faith and believe in Its power to grant any gift that will make for more efficient service in the Cause of Christ.

Such are the ones who win the "last gift," the Grace of God; they the conquerors of mind, heart, body, soul, — yea, and of Spirit.

XV. THE EYES OF THE BLIND

PAPER No. 65. MAY, 1934

IN the adjustment of human affairs, we all have much to do to preserve and save the beings of our own creation.

None other than Christ Jesus said, *"Blessed are they that have not seen, and yet have believed."* This is most true; blessed indeed is he who, having blindly and unhesitatingly put his hand in God's, follows confidently the way He leads. Praise God for him. But what will you answer to that one who in deep anguish of spirit cries. "Why—why are these things come upon me? Why? Why?"

It is to these that I address my remarks. Was it not told of Solomon, who asked for an understanding heart, that he was given, not only wisdom, but all things? Now how can an understanding heart be gained? Through prayer—yes; but something more is required. And that is the facing of your human minds—your selves, and seeing them for just what they are; and when you have a true understanding of your selves, you then have an understanding of all humanity. For is not humanity *your* creation; does it not consist of your human selves?

In other words, are you not responsible for mankind, for your own kind, your other selves.

Remember, when God looked on His creation. He called it good. Can you look upon your creation—your selves, and call them good? So I say unto you, be no longer blind but begin impartially and systematically to examine this self that you call you.

Now there always comes a time when man, having followed by faith, arrives at a place of Initiation where he is compelled to take stock of himself—as a son of God, if he would go onward and upward on the Path to the Kingdom. He then realises wherein he has fallen short, and how incapable he is now of possessing and controlling the Kingdom of which he is the heir, when he reaches it. Why is this? Having come this far, he can no longer blame, adverse circumstances and various other outer hindrances, for he knows they are of his own creation. Then the fault must lie in himself—in some quality, lack, shortcoming or weakness of his human mind.

What does a man do who suddenly finds himself the possessor of a great fortune? If he is wise, would he not immediately take stock of all that he is and has, then of what he needs and wants; and then consider how- best to invest his fortune to the greatest advantage? He would also consult others wiser than himself; but chief of all he would take stock of himself. So must you take stock of yourselves as sons of God, inheritors of your Father's Kingdom.

Let us now look on these creations—your selves. If you have come to or passed the place of the Dweller on the Threshold, you have seen and conquered the *big* faults that had prevented your going farther; just as when looking at your garden you perceive the huge weeds that stand out glaringly, and you immediately uproot them. The garden now may look fairly clean— from a distance; so you sow your additional seeds and wait expectantly for the blooming of the flowers. But what have we? Alas, a few flowers are blooming where formerly were the tall weeds; but the other seeds evidently fell among smaller and more tenacious weeds and were choked out so they could not come to bloom. Now a wise gardener would have pulled out all the weeds, ' both big and small and by carefully watching and tending his garden, would in due season have been rewarded with all the flowers of which he had dreamed.

So it is with you, aspirants on the Path; having eradicated the more glaring faults, you sit back and wonder that the blossoming of your efforts has not come in greater abundance. Now, dear ones, let us hold a mirror before your minds and see what prevents the harvest. Let us search carefully every hidden place, examine every motive, every desire, every thought, and then tear out and uproot everything that you, as sons of God, know is unworthy—all the weeds that limit and prevent your harvest of good, that prevents the manifestation of God in and through you.

Having gone so long, blind to your selves so much in evidence, this labor of extracting every tiny fault of self will prove a kneebending, heartbreaking process; but it is worth it, for have we not Jesus' promise that *"The things that I do, ye shall do, and greater than these shall ye do in My name."*

Dearly beloved, remember His Name! And what is His Name, but Love? Can you not plainly see that all the things He did you shall do, but that they will be done in the Name of LOVE? Love for God, which is also love for your fellowmen. Why should you not willingly serve your fellowmen? Are they not your own creations? Are they not what you now see them to be in your human minds? How can they change until you see and know them as they really are—in Gods image and likeness, all-loving, all-good, and all-perfect? For is not God All in all, is He not all that every man is?

The time has come when every knee shall bow and every tongue shall confess it. You, as sons of God, knowing this great truth, must now compel your human minds to know it with you—and to think, speak and act in that knowing. So it is time to be up and doing—to forget self and selfs ongoing in the redemption of your thought creations, which, affect the whole human race— as well as your human personal selves.

IT IS THIS great truth to which each one of you have been blind. You have wondered at the outward appearance of yourself. Why have you ill health, why poverty, why these defects of the flesh? The. Master was always beautiful. Why are not you the same as He? Know this, that the outer of you is but a reflection of your soul. What is your soul? It is your consciousness. What is your consciousness? It is the sum-total of the thoughts and Beliefs about yourself that you are carrying around in your mind.

Then how can you be beautiful with that ugly picture of yourself you see in your mind? How can you be perfect in body, if you are not perfect in your soul? Do you know that the human mind expresses in the body only what you believe you are in your subconsciousness?

Of course, your True Self, as a Son of God—what you are in reality— is wonderful, glorious, perfect; for you are *pure Spirit*. But if you do not have the consciousness of this, how can it express through your soul, mind and body?

Claim your heritage. Each day proclaim to your soul what you are in reality... When it becomes inbred in the soul—in your subconsciousness, it will be reflected in the mind and the body. Had the Master not known His Heritage, could He have given us the truths He gave? But of course, you say, being God He was fully conscious of His Godhood. But did not He say we were *His Brothers:'* Let us here and now accept this fact, and *act on it.*

Oh, my beloved, dwell on this day and night, and the power of the indwelling Christ Spirit shall indeed transmute this flesh and you shall become like Him—knowing Him as He is and as you really are. In the Great Universal Mind of God, you *are* perfect. SEE yourself in His likeness, instead of that picture you now see in the 'mirror of your mind; and then DO the "Things He did through the great Love He came to express to, in and through you and all of God's children. In the name of Love all things are possible. Then no longer feed with the swine, but be up and about your Father's business—Love and Service for your brothers, altogether for' setting self, thereby serving Him Who has shown you the Way.

Be not blind. Having eyes to see, see and know this great truth. We are all children of the King of Glory, Who bequeathes to you His Wisdom, His Love, and His Power.

In the foregoing, I tried to tell you of your Divinity. That if you will *eat* of Christ's body (which is Spirit), and *drink* of His blood (which is Life), which means, will SEE always as He saw and DO as He did, you will surely come into your inheritance.

To go a step farther, I say that if you will follow the teaching of the Work with which you are now affiliated, together with the reading and studying the words of the Master, Jesus Christ, following every step of the Way pointed, you can not help but come into the Kingdom. This Work (The Sun Center) reaches more hungry and thirsty *souls* than any one other teaching, because it is a Work of Love and Service and follows so closely that of the Master. And everyone who makes it possible that this Truth be more widely spread among the children of earth shall partake of the glory thereof.

You have often heard, Oh beloved, that: "As *a man thinketh in his heart, so is he.*" If I should tell you that thoughts are almost, I might say, living realities, it may help you to glimpse the meaning of these words. A thought unleashes a force, the power of which ordinary man has not the faintest idea, for the magnitude of its power for good or evil depends only on the nature of the thought.

Especially is this so in tins day, when all the dark forces are loosed on earth because man's evil thoughts, those of hatred, greed, oppression, envy, jealousy, and doubt. Could you see the effects of this terrible power used by man as they really are, you would be exceedingly careful. Not only are these effects being felt and will be felt in far greater measure in nature's reaction thereto, in the tempests, ram, floods, earthquakes, volcanoes, etc., but by the loosing of these agents of darkness, they will manifest in an even greater degree in man himself—in disease, insanity, famine and plagues.

For let me tell you, thoughts are really at the bottom of all of these— they are what bring them into manifestation. Thoughts are actually magnets that attract to them everything of their kind. Watch therefore, I pray you, and see to it that your thoughts are magnets of Love, Charity, Peace, joy and Good of all kinds, else your very thoughts turn on you as wild beasts and destroy you— their creator.

This brings us back to what was stated in the beginning of this lesson; by your thoughts shall you be known, for they can no more help outmanifesting in your body and in your life than a rose-bush can help bearing a rose, or a violet-plant a violet. It especially behooves you at this time to think as Paul said; *"Whatsoever things are true, whatsoever things are honorable, whatsoever things are lovely, whatsoever things are good, if there be any virtue, if there be any praise, think on these."* For by your thinking are you judged and do you bring judgment on the earth, on your fellowmen, and on yourself.

For it is known by many that everything manifesting in the outer is a picture, or thought in consciousness. Is there a storm, with high winds, then know that it is but the storm forces let loose in men's minds; and that they go on and on in the world of consciousness until they return to their originator, their creator—man.

NOW BELOVED, be no longer as one having eyes, yet seeing not. For though you have not seen and yet believe, I charge you now to believe that you see; and your spiritual eyes shall be opened to see the things of Reality, which are Spirit and are Truth.

This earthly vision is but an illusion, a reflection, often distorted, of the Real or "Spiritual; just as man being in reality perfect spiritually, in God's image and likeness, appears distorted in the imperfect mirror of his human mind, which seeing blindly believes in the reality of the mirage his mirror presents to his earthly eyes.

Can you not see that to worship God *in Spirit and* in *Truth* you will have to see as God sees, Who looked upon His world and called it good, very good? In the beautiful mosaic God put together, each piece is peculiarly draped and is fitted into its particular place. Man may fool himself for a time, thinking *he* has placed himself where he is. But be not deceived, man of himself had nothing to do with it, hut is so blind to the Will and Power of God that he sees his human self as *something wonderful that he* has created. Open your eyes and see that *everything* is God, *every plan* of *man* is God's plan, and all are intended for the working out and redemption of the human mind that man calls his self.

Can you not sec how the very' incompatibility of Spirit and self causes a conflict in the flesh and in outer appearances? See behind appearances. Be blind no longer, but with eyes of Truth see appearances as they are— nothing but the warring of the members (forces); and quickly get into the true consciousness that all is God, is of God, and for God.

Then see how quickly everything adjusts itself and harmony manifests everywhere; when you will truly say, "Not my will, but Thine, Oh God." And in saying this you will come into the true consciousness—

which is *pure knowing and seeing,* and you will be what you really are—God's own image and likeness.

And I promise you then that *what your Spiritual eyes see, will manifest to the outer eye.* Let him who hath eyes to see, believe in verity and truth.

Peace, and many blessings of God be upon you; and may the Spirit of Christ within bring you into oneness with Him, where you may see as He sees, no longer blinded by the delusions of the human separate mind.

OTHER PASTURES

THE ABOVE was given to one of the workers at the Sun Center, and we consider it as belonging to all who are a paw of the Work and as so important that all should receive it and thereby get the help that it provides.

It should be studied in connection with Lesson No. 64, on *Patience,* as it in a way supplements and completes its message; but we urge that each truth in it be stayed with until all of its wonderful meaning becomes clear, if you would get the benefit that awaits. You can see that these truths are given to those who have had the teachings and who are. now being called upon to put their truths to use, so that they can *soon* reach the Kingdom and enter upon their Divine Heritage.

Having eyes to see, how many of you who read have seen the inner meaning of the deep truths in these Lessons—have stayed with them until you did see, *and then set about proving them in your lives?* This has been the burden of our injunctions for sometime past, and it will be continually impressed upon you until all wake up to the need of making yourselves do what you know you should do.

For more than anything else, it seems necessary, with most of those, seeking the Kingdom, for us to stay *close to them,* individually and as a whole, until we get them one by one to see the vital importance of *making themselves do* the things suggested and what they know *must be done* to reach the goal, and until *we actually see them doing it.*

You have only to "take stock of your self" to see how true this is; and therefore you will have to bear with us - -who as your Brothers, having only the interest of our Master at heart in bringing all of His sheep into the pasture, permitting not one to loiter or stray away, so that His flock be kept intact—if we are so urgent in our efforts to keep you going forward to where He is waiting for you.

This is the task to which He has appointed us and to which we have set ourselves, and we are concerned only that we are obeying Him, knowing that He within each one of you will take care of the results, after we have done our part. What if the personality rebels, does not like thus being prodded and urged onward, and wants to escape into some enticing bypath or field? Our part is to tell them the truth, to show them the one sure and safe way.

If they still insist on following the way of personality and of self, then we must let them go—for the needed lessons that await in the disillusionment and suffering that will be theirs. Be sure He will make them see it all in His own good time and way. Not one of His sheep will ever be really lost. Blessed is He who knows that. But thrice blessed is he who seeks only to follow and please Him.

THIS perhaps is a good occasion to speak of those who have traveled with us this far, and who are also taking other courses of study, or are members of some occult order or society, or have found some teacher whose teachings are much like those of *The Impersonal Life*, and to whom they look for help and guidance. There are some of such, we regret to say—not because of the seeming defection, but because they are like those of the Maker's fold who think they ₁au find more and better pasture elsewhere, and while they would follow Him and love the Impersonal teachings through which He led them, yet they do not want to miss what these other pastures provide.

So they are dividing their energies, even after partaking of all the Spiritual food—eating of Christ's body, seeing Who Christ really is—that He is the Only Begotten Son of God *in every man,* the actual SELF of every man, the one and only Teacher who can and will teach them all things and lead them unto all truth— when they turn to Him in perfect faith and trust.

We know that such seemingly could not truly have understood this wonderful Revelation, or they would not have sought elsewhere for what can only be found within: for the way to find it surely was shown them in the Impersonal teachings.

What more are they seeking? Occult powers, a quicker way to self mastery, a *personal* Master or Teacher? Have they so missed the vital essence of *The Impersonal Life,* and the truths of Jesus Christ?

O beloved, if you would only study and stay with the great truths in the Lessons sent you until you get all of their inner meaning, you would not have the desire or the inclination to wander into other pastures—you would truly turn *within* and let Christ lead you all the way, and you would be concerned with no other thing but that you were listening to His Voice only, and were leaving self and its subtle temptations far behind.

We have had several write us in similar vein to the words of one who said, "I now know that God—Christ is here on earth in a *bodily form,* to bless and save all mankind. He is the True Principle and I know it. I thank you Father."

We wrote, reminding her of the great truth that God is All in *all,* "that He cannot therefore be in just one man, and must be as much in you as He is in any man of earth. Above all things have you been taught not to look to a personality, but to seek and look only to the Loving Christ *within.* Did not our Dear Master say in ʳ words so plain that it must make you stop and think,

"Call no man your father upon the earth; for one is your Father, which is in Heaven. Neither be ye called masters; for one is your Master, even Christ."

"Yet you are looking to an earthly man to be God, when God is All *in all.* Even Jesus had to go away from His disciples and from the world because the world insisted upon worshipping Him, the *man,* and thereby failed to find Christ and God within themselves. Have all your studies and all His teachings and your Faith in Him been for naught? Think, dear sister, before you lose yourself altogether in the illusion that is now enshrouding your mind. We are here only to help our dear ones, and we send you these words of living truth for your help."

Those who are trying to study other teachings while they are a part of this Work, will find that they are but scattering their forces and that they will be unable to make any headway Spiritually; for they are but dallying – and have strayed aside into other pastures. As their acknowledged shepherd we must point them "back" to the true way.

If they still prefer their own way, it were far better that they separate from this Work and concentrate upon the other teachings until they get from them what they want. Those only *belong* in this *Impersonal* Work who are no longer seeking anything for self but who are making the finding of the Kingdom *first* and *supreme* in their hearts and lives, and who are preparing themselves for Christ's service.

We know this after long experience—-that no one can divide his interest and his. energies and get anywhere. Thereto! ₜ it behooves with to take stock of themselves to see *just what it is they are seeking, so* they no longer deceive, themselves into believing they are truly seeking the Kingdom—when something else is first in their minds.

A CHANGE FROM THE PAPERS

Because of a situation that has arisen as a result of the new printer's and linotyper's code recently put into effect by the Government, causing us to face the necessity of paying nearly twice as much as formerly for the printing of the monthly Paper and the INNER LIFE Magazine, we have given much consideration to just what was best to do to meet the issue.

We finally decided to lessen the cost of production of the Magazine by using cheaper cover stock and smaller type, thereby giving room for more contents and enabling us to have an Impersonal Work Department and include therein each month the material intended for the Paper, thus combining the two, and sending the Magazine, beginning with the June number, instead of the Paper.

This would give all those receiving the current Paper the advantage of receiving not only the monthly Impersonal message, but all the valuable truths in the Magazine, which will be found to be very helpful, even if not as advanced as those in the Impersonal Department.

In view of this change, we trust that all those who have been with us so long will not miss the Paper, but will be glad thus to co-operate and to help us secure many new subscribers for the Magazine.

For despite the fact that the Magazine is costing more to produce than formerly, we are reducing the subscription price from $2.50 to $1.50 per year, feeling that the truths in it are so important that they should be brought within the reach of every possible earnest seeker. Therefore, with the help of its friends and of those who are a real part of the Work and who wish to have it grow so that many thousands can receive of its benefits, it is hoped and believed that with this reduced price the subscription list and sales will in time be built up so that the loss of two-fifths of the income will soon be made up. To this end we do not hesitate to ask the support of all who have the interest of the Work at heart.

Please understand that this offer is only for those who have received sixty-five Papers, or who have traveled with us from the beginning so they are getting this May Paper. All others wishing the magazine will of course subscribe for it in the usual way.

Those who are already subscribers will be the ones who will not get the full benefit of this change—from a monetary standpoint, because, there are quite a number who were not subscribers who will now receive the Magazine without extra cost.

But as all who have come with us this far are not in the Work for what they can get out of it, but for what they can do to help it grow and thereby to bless many more others; and as nearly all are now supporting the Work as their hearts dictate, we feel that former Magazine subscribers will be only too glad to aid further in this way, and those, receiving it without cost will be inspired to assist more than ever before, because of learning what a wonderful medium of helpfulness is the Magazine.

THE end.

Made in the USA
San Bernardino, CA
04 April 2019